Amy,

Continue to Be Kind...

and Live from your Heart!

Doug ♥

POWER
FROM THE
HEART

A collection
of inspiring stories and insights
that will
Ignite Your Soul

DOUG DAVIDSON

Power from the Heart

A collection of inspiring stories and insights that will *Ignite Your Soul*

ISBN: 978-1-7367698-3-6 (Hardcover)
ISBN: 978-1-7367698-1-2 (Paperback)
ISBN: 978-1-7367698-2-9 (E-Book)

Library of Congress Control Number: 2021905940

Cover design by Cherie Foxley at www.cheriefox.com
Cover background photo by Matt Marshall Photography
Cover portrait photo by Jill Jones Photography

Printed in the United States of America

Power from the Heart Publishing
1350 San Pablo Drive
San Marcos, CA 92078

For more information on this book, the author and programs offered by Power from the Heart, visit: www.PowerFromTheHeart.net or email: Doug@PowerFromTheHeart.net

I dedicate this book to my wife, Janice Davidson. She is the love of my life.

We have enjoyed many great times together and she has also stood with me through some dark times in my life. Janice is someone I can count on no matter what. There is not a more giving, selfless, and hard-working person on the planet.

I so appreciate her for creating the space for me to spend countless hours writing this book, while taking care of a multitude of things so I could stay focused. Never once did she complain of the time spent; rather she continually supported me in my goal to create a lasting legacy through this book.

Janice Davidson
(Jill Jones Photography)

TABLE OF CONTENTS

ACKNOWLEDGEMENTS

Martin Rutte

"You have to do it yourself, and you can't do it alone"

– Martin Rutte, Founder,
ProjectHeavenOnEarth.com

I have been thinking of writing this book for a long time. I awoke at 3:33 a.m. on March 24, 2020 and the title of the book came to me. I got up and wrote it down. It was the beginning of putting pen to paper.

I want to thank the countless supporters who have encouraged me to write this book and have been involved in the process along the way. Some have spent many hours editing and giving feedback, some were an inspiration for a story, while others believed in me and encouraged me to see this book through to completion. You all played a vital role and I thank you from the bottom of my very full heart.

This partial list includes Bruce Hurd, who showed up with his magical book-writing course, *Make Your Book A Reality*, at the perfect time. Not only did his course give me a great foundation for writing, his hours of coaching and editing were essential to getting this book published. I hope I do you proud.

My dearest friends Mark and Bridget Wright, who inspire me daily.

The many mentors and coaches from whom I learned so much in my early years when I was formulating my values. They include my high school coaches, Doug Staniforth and Steve Jackson. They taught me to always give my best effort, no matter what.

Later, I gained lifetimes of experience in a few short years working with business and personal development leaders that include Werner Erhard, Stewart Emery, Martin Rutte, Raymond Aaron, Tony Robbins, and Mark Victor Hansen.

Special acknowledgments to all my team members at The Davidson Group Realty: Janice Davidson, Tyler Davidson, Ben Humbert, and Jason Daniels who have covered for me while I took on this project. And to Jamie Fleming, Liliana Riquer, Steven "Chief" Kuryla, and my brother and sister-in-law, Jim and Julie Davidson, who have constantly encouraged me to complete this book.

Thank you to the talented Ben Humbert for his artwork and for his inspiration to use the photo on the front cover of the book.

Thank you to Denise Cassino of BestSellerServices.com for guiding me through the publishing and book-launch process.

Finally, I wish to thank all the clients and friends who have made such a huge contribution to my life in ways you may never understand. Without you there would be no story to tell.

I also dedicate this book to my sons, Tyler and Graham, who I live for to inspire. I hope that some of the insights I have gained will serve them well and they will not have to make as many mistakes as I have along this journey called life.

———————♡———————

FOREWORD BY MARK WRIGHT

I am an Executive Leadership Coach and have had the privilege to partner up with thousands of clients over the past 25-years. This has provided me with the opportunity to glean insights and understanding into the values, character, and integrity of the human spirit.

Only on exceedingly rare occasions someone shows up who stands head and shoulders above the crowd of humanity. One of those individuals is my dear friend, Doug Davidson.

My wife and I met Doug and Janice shortly after we migrated from Australia to USA, 27 years ago. Doug took us under his wing and guided and supported us as we transitioned into life in America. Doug's generosity, kindness, and selfless service has been the cornerstone of our friendship.

Doug is one of the most loving, compassionate, generous-hearted human beings I have ever met in my life. He is constantly seeking opportunities as to how he can be of selfless service to others. He demonstrates and lives integrity at a level I have only observed by a few people.

Doug is one of the most highly respected, integral human beings I know. He personifies integrity in how he chooses to live his life.

A few years ago, my wife broke her neck in a bicycle accident. After sharing this news with Doug, he asked me if I was "alright," to which I responded "Yes." However, he immediately booked a flight from San Diego to Lake Tahoe, to meet me at the hospital and arrived the next day to support me during this crisis. Even though I thought I was OK, his caring, support and being there for both my wife and I was truly an action of Selfless Service. Doug personally emailed all our family and friends, individually, to update them on my wife's progress, and responded to the many incoming emails. Doug's compassionate action during our time of need personifies his generosity, thoughtfulness, and kindheartedness.

Doug is truly an incredible person who "*walks his talk*".

When Doug shared the news that he had committed to writing a book of his life's experiences, insights, learnings, and understandings, I was truly delighted. Now, more than ever, humanity needs a guiding light to open up their hearts and minds, to live their lives more fully and purposefully.

Doug's compelling writing style exudes directly from his heart. He opens up his life to reveal his insights in the hope that we can glean and personally learn from these powerful, inspiring stories.

The insights and the challenges provided in his book are a roadmap for us to learn, grow and develop ourselves to our full potential.

Mark Wright
The Integrity Coach

INTRODUCTION

Here I am at Lake San Marcos, CA, 2017
(Jill Jones Photography)

*"If you want to make the world a better place,
take a look at yourself and then make a change."*

– from "Man in The Mirror,"
Michael Jackson, Grammy Lifetime Achievement Award

Have you ever wondered what it would be like to start a new career, just because you're inspired to change your life in a completely new direction? What about competing in the grueling IRONMAN Triathlon World Championships in Hawaii? Or conquering a life-long fear of public speaking, to become a highly sought-after motivational speaker? And how about dropping everything to become a professional golfer (at age 44, no less)?

I've done all of these things and so much more. In this book I share, from my heart, my most inspiring and emotional experiences – good and bad, successful and unsuccessful.

At the end of each story, I share the insights and lessons I have learned from each experience.

Most of my insights are from successes. Others are a result of extremely difficult situations I found myself in, and the painful decisions I needed to make. I share what I learned during my amazing adventures, so you may apply the same lessons in your own wonderful life.

Mostly, though, I want to help you understand that you are in control of your own life, simply by the powerful choices you make. You can make it as adventurous and fulfilling as you want it to be. You don't have to be Superman or Superwoman. You just have to believe in yourself and see how incredibly worthy you are. Let me help you do just that.

All of the insights I share have helped guide me throughout my life. As you read on, you will learn more about me, my values, and my true soul.

My goal is that the stories will ignite your soul and inspire you to live your life to the fullest.

I was born in Montreal, Canada on December 7, 1956. With the exception of a few years travelling as a child, I lived in Canada until I was 38 years old, when I moved to the United States. I finally settled in the San Diego, CA area and now have my U.S. citizenship.

I learned most of my values at a young age from my parents, Willard and Doreen Davidson. My parents were both supportive and strict at the same time. I was taught solid values that included: treat others how I would want to be treated, always do my best, complete every job I start, and never take shortcuts. They sure gave me a great foundation to build on.

Sports became a big part of my life and kept me out of trouble in school. In fact, on many days it was only a practice or a game that motivated me to go to school. I found school pretty boring; sports helped me get through it.

My confidence level growing up was pretty low but over time, with small victories, it grew and grew. As you will learn through the stories, I also had my share of setbacks, humbling experiences, and on more than one occasion I had to completely rebuild my life from nothing.

I was not born with a silver spoon in my mouth – everything I have was earned. I spent a good part of my early life in survival mode. Out of necessity I was focused on myself, doing everything I could just to pay my bills. As a result, I was not able to make any significant contribution to others. It was only later in life, around age 50, that I truly got in touch with what I believe is my true purpose: "To inspire others."

Once I realized this, and I put my attention on serving others, money started to flow to me. Now I am in philanthropy mode. My focus is no longer on myself, but rather on how much of a contribution I can make to others. Nothing gives me more satisfaction than being able to give back to others and watching them grow.

This collection of stories is a true reflection of my purpose. I sincerely hope you enjoy reading the stories, and that they provide you with inspiration and real tools to develop your own Power from the Heart.

1

LEARNING FROM THE MASTER – TONY ROBBINS

Tony Robbins performing on stage

"If you want to be successful, find someone who has achieved the results you want and copy what they do, and you'll achieve the same results."

– Tony Robbins, World's #1 Success Coach

T he night before the seminar the driver picked me up at my place in a huge white stretch limo. We headed to the airport to pick up none other than Tony Robbins, author of

Unlimited Power and *Awaken the Giant Within* and world-renowned motivational speaker. I was so excited I could barely stand it.

I had the driver wait in the limo at the curb and I went inside to the baggage area to meet Tony. No need for one of those cheesy signs limo drivers hold up when they have no idea who they are picking up. Tony was larger than life and could easily be spotted in a crowd.

I waited anxiously, worried about being "star struck." When he finally arrived, I greeted him and shook his huge hand. I am 6-foot-1 and I felt dwarfed by Tony who stands at 6-foot-7. I introduced myself and said my limo was parked outside. When we reached the limo, I opened the back door, he folded himself in and stretched out his long legs. Then I got in and sat across from him on the white-leather seat.

The look on his face was priceless. He thought I was the limo driver!

"Who is driving?" Tony asked.

At that point I knocked on the privacy window and instructed the limo driver to take us to the hotel. It was the beginning of an incredible 24 hours.

Some months earlier I had asked myself, "What is the fastest way to achieve my wildest dreams? And how can I do it without all the struggle, setbacks, anxiety, and heartbreaking failure that go along with achieving greatness?"

The answer was simple. Find myself a mentor. Someone who has already done what I wanted to do. A master of his craft.

I needed a mentor who could share with me how to achieve the success I wanted, and more importantly what NOT to do, to avoid the failure I dreaded. A mentor could catapult me to success and save me years of heartache, anxiety and countless dollars spent in the wrong places. My mentor could be my personal guide along the way.

Then I asked myself, "How do I find a mentor – and how do I approach him?" Tony Robbins was the man who I wanted to emulate.

In 1995, I was living in the tiny town of Vancouver, Washington, just across the river from Portland, Oregon. I had just started a small seminar company called *Business Transitions International*. I was teaching a series of courses for budding entrepreneurs. I taught them how to find or create a business they loved, the mechanics of how to run it, and how to market themselves effectively on a shoe-string budget. I was experienced at that because I had started my business with absolutely no money. The business was doing okay, but just barely paying the bills; life at that time was not easy for me.

When I say a small business, I mean really small – the total number of employees was one – me! I had no other employees and had volunteers help me during the seminars. Running the business meant doing everything from creating marketing materials, stuffing envelopes, enrolling people on the phone, being my own "roadie" and setting up seminar rooms and chairs, lugging in the sound system – everything. I was doing what I loved but kept searching for ways to improve. Since I was the teacher and not the student, there wasn't anyone to ask.

At that time, Tony Robbins was easily the most successful seminar leader on the planet – there wasn't even a close second. He was "The Master" (and still is). He was selling out huge venues, consulting with world leaders, and advising professional sports teams. It seemed every time I turned on the TV, his infomercials were running.

I had already read all of Tony's books and listened to his Personal Power series of audio tapes over and over. He was clearly where I wanted to be. But how could I reach him? Why would he want to mentor me? What did I have to offer him? I was busting my butt to get 30 people in a seminar; he was a household name.

Tony lived in the famous Del Mar Castle perched high on the bluff overlooking the Pacific Ocean. I was living in a small apartment in Vancouver, Washington struggling to pay the rent. These were the thoughts I was holding in my mind.

I learned long ago that if I don't ask for what I want, the answer is always "no." So, I mustered up my courage and tried calling his office, only to be screened by two layers of people. I never got through to Tony.

Then one day the tide changed. I was reading our local newspaper and saw an ad for a Tony Robbins seminar happening in Portland. It started the very next week, so I immediately enrolled. I thought this was my chance to meet Tony – I was so excited. The next week I went to the seminar. What a letdown!

It was being run by two people who had bought a Tony Robbins franchise. They had purchased the rights to run seminars using a video presentation of Tony. Every 20 minutes or so they would stop the video and we would turn to a workbook. They were nice people, excellent facilitators, and the seminar was quite effective, but certainly not the same as having Tony in the room.

I was so disappointed. But then my mind started wandering and I thought, *What if I had other people leading my seminars all around the world?* That would be some incredible leverage.

Still, I remained committed to meeting Tony Robbins. I got to know the franchisees and invited them to take my seminars. We started to build a relationship. I then shared with them that I wanted to meet Tony and asked if they could set that up for me. They said, "Doug we bought one of his franchises and we don't even get to talk to him – good luck with that dream."

A month later they came to my class, excited to announce that Tony was coming to Portland in a couple of months and would be giving a one-day seminar at the convention center. Most of the people in my class rushed to buy tickets.

After that class I approached the seminar leaders again. I figured since Tony was going to be right in our town it would be relatively easy for them to introduce me to him. Again, they said it was a pipe dream. They would be introducing him from the stage and that was it. His schedule was completely full, from the time he arrived to the moment he left.

I felt I had to get creative. I knew from his books that Tony worked out every day and would need a place to exercise when he was there. I assumed he would likely want some privacy, instead of a bunch of people wanting his autograph. There was a gym in the apartment complex where I lived. I approached the manager to see if they could close it for an hour for Tony's personal use. The manager got permission to do so. I called the franchise owners and told them I had it all set up. They appreciated my efforts but said his schedule was already full. He would likely be working out at the hotel where he was staying.

On to Plan B. The next day I called the franchise owners to see if I could pick Tony up at the airport. They said they would be arranging a limousine company that would be picking him up in exchange for two tickets to his seminar. I said let me take care of it. Since we had already established a good relationship, they trusted me enough to take this on, and it freed up one item from their long list of things to do to prepare for such a huge event. I got the name of the limo company and called them. I paid for the biggest stretch limo available, and I got the two front-row tickets to Tony's seminar from the franchise owners.

During the 20-minute ride to the hotel, Tony and I instantly hit it off. I shared with Tony my dream of meeting him and how I made the arrangements to pick him up. I took a few moments to really acknowledge Tony for what he had accomplished in his life. Then I asked if he would mind if I asked him a question. He was startled by this person sitting across from him, but was incredibly gracious and said, "Ask any question you want."

My first question was, "How do you fill a convention center with thousands of people?" He answered that question and then the information started to flow like a river. He didn't hold anything back. Tony shared with me step-by-step how he recorded his best-selling Personal Power tapes that I had almost memorized. He shared how he prepares for a seminar before he goes on stage. Anything I wanted to know was freely given. That information was priceless, and it was all just handed to me. I was soaking everything up as fast as it was coming. It was clear that Tony was happy to share his secrets, and he had only known me for a few minutes. What an incredibly generous human being.

The next morning, Tony needed to get from the hotel to the convention center so once again I was his "driver." We spent another 15 minutes in the limo. As we arrived at the convention center Tony invited me to spend the day with him. He said, "Come on backstage with me as I prepare, have lunch with me and my staff and then you can take me back to the airport." I couldn't believe this was happening. I could not make this stuff up. There is no way to explain how things like this happen, other than I had a clear intention of what I wanted, and I was willing to ask for it.

I went backstage with Tony and he began preparing himself by visualizing and doing some deep breathing exercises to get his energy up. In my entire life, I had never witnessed anyone so intense and focused. There was an aura radiating from him like a golden glow.

During this time frame, the audience was pouring into the sold-out convention center. There was a massive stage erected, with a sound system fit for a rock concert blaring music to energize the crowd. Of course, Tony did not have to sell any tickets, or set up the room. This allowed him simply to focus on delivering his message. This was the big show. I got a ring-side seat and a back-stage pass.

A few minutes later, the franchise owners climbed up the stairs to the stage, got everyone's attention and made a few announcements. Because Tony was so famous, there really was no need for any introduction. Within seconds, Tony bounded on to the stage and shook hands with the hosts, who quickly left the stage. After spending a lot of money to purchase a franchise, the only interaction they had with him was a few fleeting seconds as they passed him on stage. I was with Tony all day, from the time I picked him up in the morning to the time he stepped on the plane to return. I felt bad for the Portland franchise owners who had no other contact with their mentor the entire time he was in Portland.

As expected, the seminar was exceptional. Tony is clearly a master at his craft and deserves everything he has earned. I learned so much from him by observing, by asking more questions, by watching how the seminar was orchestrated and by talking to his staff at lunch. It was an experience that provided me with years of hard-earned wisdom – simply by spending time with Tony for just one day. And the best part was that aside from renting the limo, it didn't cost me anything. All I had to do was be creative and ask.

Tony gave his all that day and went well past the scheduled finish time. He gave the audience everything it could have hoped for and more. After he finished, my job was to get him to the airport for his flight back to San Diego. Considering the distance and the traffic, I could tell it was going to be tight. Then I witnessed something I have never seen before. From the limo, Tony called the airlines to tell them he would be up to 10 minutes late and asked them to hold the plane for him. He put on a pair of running shoes while he sat in the limo so he could run to the gate. He handed me his enormous, size 16 dress shoes and asked if I would ship them back to him. (They required a big box!) Once we arrived at the airport he was gone in a flash. A few days after I shipped his shoes to him, I received a "Thank You" in the mail along with one of his autographed books.

A few months later, I was teaching "How to Attract a Mentor" in my seminar and shared with my audience the story of how I met Tony. One of the participants had just returned from taking Tony's week-long Mastery course in Hawaii. He was excited to share how Tony spoke about how he had met me in Portland during that event. Evidently, we made an equally strong impression on each other.

Fast forward to January 2021. My wife, Janice, and I enrolled in a Tony Robbins virtual seminar called *New World, New You, Challenge*. Tony had to adapt to doing a virtual seminar as he could not do a live seminar during this time of COVID-19. Amazingly he attracted 832,000 participants online from 195 countries for a five-day course. Tony took a problem and turned into a massive opportunity. He continues to grow by leaps and bounds and has definitely earned the title of World's #1 Success Coach. I am so grateful to have spent a day with him.

———————————— ♡ ————————————

What insights did I gain from this experience?

If I don't ask – the answer is always no.

If I keep asking for what I want and continue searching for how to receive it, eventually the answer will become "yes." Sometimes I just need to be a little more creative in order to receive what I am committed to.

Most phenomenally successful people want to give back and it gives them great joy to do so.

Giving back seems to be human nature for evolved human beings. There is an innate desire in us to give back and help others. That is where people get the greatest joy. I have learned that by asking for help, I am actually offering someone a gift – the opportunity to give back.

You can gain a lifetime of experience from a mentor in an incredibly short period of time.

I learned so much from Tony in just one day. Gaining his wealth of knowledge and experience helped me tremendously to build a successful seminar business. I also learned I did not want to lead the life he was living. Tony's schedule, and the demands on him were way too intense for me. So, while I was gaining knowledge from a Master, I was also learning a valuable life lesson. I selected that which worked for my life – not his.

———————————— ♡ ————————————

If you are committed to attracting a Master Mentor,
you may want to consider using my method to connect
with them – it worked wonders for me.

- Do your homework and choose the person who can best help you achieve your dreams.

- Reach out to them by letter or phone first. Email is too easy to ignore.

- Acknowledge them first for their success and then ask for their help.

- Ask for one piece of advice.

- Take the advice and experiment with it.

- Now here is the critical part: report back to them on how their advice worked (or didn't work). Thank them again for their advice and ask if it would be okay to ask another question. Before you know it, you will have a lifetime friend.

- Stay humble. Remember, you are the student, so learn to LISTEN instead of speaking.

- In this situation, it is much more important to understand what you "do NOT know" and what you want to learn, than it is to stay in the comfort and security of what you already know.

2
EMBRACING RISKS

My parents, Doreen and Willard Davidson

*"If you are not willing to risk the unusual,
you will have to settle for the ordinary."*

– Jim Rohn, American Entrepreneur,
Author, and Personal Development Legend

The bully came after me again – pushing me, taunting me, and calling me names. I was scared stiff. I mustered up all my courage and gave him a good punch to the face and broke his glasses. I got a detention after school that day, but it was totally worth it. I felt like I was 10 feet tall. I stood up for myself and was never bothered by that bully again. I honestly believe that was a real turning point in my life and my confidence began to grow.

My parents imparted solid foundational values to me growing up. They also provided many great learning opportunities for me: we lived in Nigeria for three years, they sent me to a boarding school in England for a year, and we traveled extensively throughout Europe, Canada, and the United States throughout my childhood.

Elementary school was a challenging time for me. Until the day I stood up for myself, I would often get bullied in the schoolyard during recess and did not have many friends.

One day while in grade five, I confided in my Dad that I was being bullied. Going to school was so traumatic for me and I simply dreaded being there. Dad set up a punching bag in the basement and taught me how to make a fist and protect myself. He emphasized I should never instigate a fight and made it clear that being a bully myself would not be tolerated. By showing me how to protect myself, though, he gave me the courage to confront that bully who was making my life miserable.

I was extremely self-conscious as a child. I was one of the few kids who had to wear glasses. I had buck teeth and spoke with a lisp. I had to have braces on my teeth to correct that. My parents made sure that my brother and I kept our hair cut super short – the best way to describe it would be a "bean-shave." I hated going to the barber shop. And to top it all off, I was very skinny. It seemed that no matter how much I ate I could not put on any weight. My self-confidence was extremely low.

I was born and raised in Montreal, Canada. My parents, Willard and Doreen, met at the Macdonald College campus, an annex of McGill University, where they both obtained teachers' degrees. Macdonald College is in the quaint French Canadian town of Ste. Anne De Bellevue on the west island of Montreal. They were married shortly after graduating and bought a small home where I grew up, along with my younger brother and sister.

My Dad was a good-looking man who towered over us at 6-foot-3 and weighed in at 230 pounds. His size alone struck fear into us as kids and so discipline was never a problem. He was a star athlete in college, earning seven letters in football and basketball. He would have had eight if not for an injury.

My mother was a loving person who always put others before herself. She was a tireless worker and always had time for us. As my Dad was often working, Mom was at every hockey and football game possible and always had meals ready for us when we came home, tired from practice or a game. She was also a great confidant for me whenever I had challenges.

I never met anyone who had anything negative to say about my parents. Everyone loved them. They were all about giving and were always fair. Without me realizing it at the time, they served as great examples of integrity.

After I was born, my Mom stopped teaching and stayed home to raise me. Three years later my brother Jim was born; four years after that, my sister Heather was born. Mom also looked after our neighbors' kids and it was common to have six kids at the house for lunch. We went through a lot of Kraft Dinners in those days. This was long before "daycare" was a thing, and she did it to bring in some extra money. My Dad soon transitioned from being a teacher to a school principal and obtained his master's degree in education while continuing to work full time.

We lived in a tiny two-story home that only had one and a half bathrooms. It had a tiny yard and was fewer than 100 yards from the highway and close to the railway tracks. There was a four-unit apartment building next door and we were certain they were selling drugs out of there. Now, as a Realtor, I can say it was not an ideal location, but I did not pay any attention to it at the time.

The great thing was we lived only three blocks from school so I could walk and not have to take a school bus.

My Childhood Home – 1961

Living on an educator's salary caused my parents to be very frugal. Although we never wanted for anything, money was always tight. During the school year, my parents rented out a room to college students to help pay for the home mortgage. To put things in perspective, I remember how excited my Dad was when he finally paid off the mortgage in 1981. I later found out that mortgage was only $20,000.

Whenever we had renters, I was relegated to the basement, or to the tiny sunroom on the back of the house that had no insulation. Neither were great options. I hated that experience. The basement was dark and musty, and I would often get awakened by the furnace turning on in the middle of the night. In summers, I would move up to the sunroom as it was way too cold to stay in during the winter. I remember there being a constant line up in the mornings to use the only shower before heading to school.

My Dad always encouraged us to get involved in sports and by the time I was four years old, I was playing organized hockey. We played on an outdoor rink down the street that my Dad and some of the other fathers would maintain. It was a lot of work, and as there was no Zamboni (the ice-making machines you see in hockey arenas), the rink was shoveled by hand and watered at night with a fire hose. It was a real community effort to make it work. Every time it snowed the process was repeated.

There was also a small shack beside the rink where we would go to warm up. Inside there was a wood-burning stove in the middle that we would put our hat and mitts on to dry them off from the snow and warm them up. One of my most vivid memories of that rink is from a school day where it was so cold that the school buses would not start, and school was cancelled. We spent the whole day playing hockey outside and got a little frost bite on our cheeks. True Canadians.

The Winter Club – Ste. Anne De Bellevue, Quebec, Canada
(Colin Legault)

From kindergarten to grade six, school was rather uneventful. I did okay with my grades, but no subjects really excited me. I began to excel in hockey and in grade six was asked to play Junior B hockey for Westlake (an elite youth team). I can still feel how proud I was to wear the red team jacket with the Westlake crest across the front and my number 15 stitched on the sleeve. For a 10-year-old kid, that was super exciting. Growing up in Canada where hockey is the number one sport, most kids dream of playing in the National Hockey League. Playing for Westlake was getting me one step closer to that childhood fantasy.

The day I finally got my braces off my teeth, I had a hockey game. As I went into a corner a player butt-ended me with his stick right in my mouth. I was wearing a mouth-guard and the force from the stick split it in half. My lip was cut badly but fortunately my teeth were all intact. Since my lip was cut, I was bleeding all over my white jersey. My Dad was on the other side of the rink at the time and I never saw him move so fast. He was super concerned for my well-being. I am sure he was also concerned about my teeth and the huge investment he had made in my braces, which I realized later was a big stretch on their budget.

Nearing the end of grade six, Dad came down to my room in the basement one night with some big news. He announced he had just been hired into an exciting, adventurous new job. We were moving to Africa at the end of the summer, where we would be living in the country of Nigeria.

What a shocker that was. I had no idea what to make of it. I was nervous, scared, and apprehensive. But my Dad seemed excited about it and did not seem scared, so at some level I knew I was going to be okay. I remember asking him if there were going to be snakes and lions there. He sensed my apprehension and assured me we would be safe. After living there, I can attest there were indeed snakes and lions there and many other factors that put us in harm's way – but we came out relatively unscathed.

My Dad had applied to CIDA, the Canadian International Development Agency, for a job where he would be training teachers. When he applied, he had no idea where he would be posted. He had hoped for Hawaii but got Nigeria. A few months after Dad broke the news to me, we packed up our stuff and went on a three-year long adventure. None of us had any idea what we were getting into and certainly were not prepared.

Living in Nigeria could be challenging and disorienting during the best of circumstances – everything was so different from what we were used to in Canada. Instead, we moved there during the most difficult time in the country's history: we arrived during the Biafran War. The Biafran War was a brutal civil war that lasted from 1967 to 1970, when the tribal region of Biafra was trying to secede from Nigeria and become an independent country. The war was horrible in so many ways. In addition to more than 100,000 military casualties on both sides, more than two million Biafrans died from starvation and disease. This was one of the great humanitarian tragedies of the 20th Century and it affected life in Nigeria tremendously, even in places far removed from the conflict such as where we lived.

I remember, like it was yesterday, getting off the plane at the Lagos International Airport. Lagos was the capital of Nigeria, and the airport was the major port of entry into the country. The plane was parked on the tarmac and we had to go down a long set of stairs to walk into the airport. The heat was intense and so was the humidity. The smells were very strange and different to me. There were at least six men from the Nigerian Army in full combat gear, with machine guns, pointing straight at us as we got off the plane. Not the most welcoming sight. We were all scared. What the heck were we doing here? We went through customs and had all our luggage completely searched. We had not learned yet how the corrupt system worked there. We later learned that a 20-pound note given to the customs officer would have prevented all that hassle.

We stayed in a hotel waiting for our orders from CIDA and were eventually posted to Kano, in the northern part of Nigeria. Kano was just a day's drive south of the Sahara Desert and was extremely hot and dry. I found out later we were only 800 miles from the front lines of the Biafran War. The communication systems where we lived were so bad the rest of the civilized world received more news of the war than we did. And the pictures of the starving Biafran kids with the extended bellies that were featured in the news were something we saw in real life every day. Living in a third-world country sure shifted my perspective on life.

The weather was a whole new experience, as well. It was not uncommon for temperatures to reach 130 degrees. In the dry season, the dust storms were so intense we could be inside and not be able to see across the street. Within minutes after a storm started, we could write our names in the dust that settled on the table. It was so fine we could not stop the dust from coming inside. Then in the rainy season the torrential rains were beyond my imagination. When it rained, we did not even think of going outside. Within minutes, the six-foot deep ditches on either side of the roads would fill up and spill on to the roads, making them impassable. Canada has its own extreme weather, but the extreme weather changes in Nigeria were well beyond anything I had ever experienced.

Dad was working at the Kano Teachers College, which was set up by The Ohio State University. Initially we lived in a flat above the Dutch-owned KLM Airlines office in the city. The college had built a compound of about a dozen houses for the staff and we were invited to move in. The American families embraced us and soon we started to feel settled and part of a community again.

Living in Nigeria was our first experience of being both an ethnic and racial minority, and we sure stood out. Our hair was so blond it was almost white and with our bright blue eyes we were quite a contrast to the Nigerians whose hair, skin, and eyes were very dark.

Everything was so different there. It was a complete culture shock. Just everyday things we take for granted, like going to the grocery store and buying ice cream, did not exist. There was one grocery store there, but the shelves were mostly empty. With the war going on, many things were not available. One of the ironies was we could not buy peanut butter and yet more peanuts (or groundnuts as they call them in Nigeria) are grown there than almost anywhere else in the world. In the fields on the side of the roads we would see massive pyramids of peanuts in 100-pound bags stacked over 30 feet high waiting to be exported. We burned out more than one blender making our own peanut butter.

Pyramids of peanuts ready for export – Kano, Nigeria

Most of our food was purchased in the open market where the flies and smells would nauseate me.

The teachers from Ohio State who had been there for a while taught us how to survive. While certainly a foreign concept for us, my parents soon hired a staff of four out of necessity. We had a full-time cook, which was the most prestigious job. He did most of the shopping in the market with my Mom. Everything had to be bartered for and we all quickly learned that skill. We learned we needed to communicate in their language, or we would quickly be taken advantage of.

Once the groceries were brought home, all the fruits and vegetables had to be soaked in a disinfectant called Dettol, which left an after-taste on everything. Our water had to be boiled and filtered before we could drink it. Chickens were bought live and had to be killed and plucked before cooking. No such thing as chicken nuggets there. My brother and I had fun as we chased my younger sister with a chicken claw. Nothing was easy about buying food and preparing meals, and so a full-time cook proved essential. Our cook's name was Isa and he always had a big smile.

Next was Hassan, our "House Boy," according to the job title. He did all the house cleaning, laundry, and ironing. He, too, had a great attitude and was always smiling.

We had a part-time gardener who sadly ended up dying of cholera when the cholera outbreak hit the area in 1970. Cholera is an endemic and seasonal disease that occurs annually, mostly during the rainy season and more often in areas with poor sanitation. It was scary going to the market only to see people being carried out on stretchers. Local residents were dying in great numbers and the government didn't have the resources or expertise and no one knew enough about the disease to control it. It was tragic and disturbing to witness.

While our gardener was still alive, there was not much grass to cut, as most of the year it was too dry for much to grow. We had a poinsettia tree in front of our house that bloomed bright red at Christmas. Of course, all the vegetation there was completely different from what I was used to as it adapted to the hot, dry climate.

We also hired a night watchman. He was essential or we would have been robbed blind – in fact, we were robbed once in bright daylight before he was hired. He was a nomadic Tuareg from the Sahara Desert and did not speak a word of English. He always wore a long flowing robe and full head-dress. His weapon was a sword that was so sharp you could shave with it. He had a peg leg, one arm, three fingers on his good hand, and nobody would mess with him. He would show up at dusk with his straw mat and his tiny tea pot and cup and park himself in front of the garage. He would make a tiny fire to boil his tea. I will never forget watching that process. As the coals would burn down, he would use his bare hands to rearrange them and never got burned. As he sat there in the dark, "cross-legged" with his good leg and his stump, all you could see were the whites of his eyes.

Our staff of four cost about $20 a week. It was here I learned about treating everyone as equals. Nigeria had been a British colony that had gained its independence in 1960, but the British expatriates still treated the Nigerians as servants. My parents, on the contrary, treated our staff like they were part of our family. My Dad always paid them more than everyone else, treated them with dignity, and was quick to take their kids to the doctor when needed. My parents bought them clothes regularly, too. My parents and our staff had a mutual respect and sincere appreciation for each other. As a result, we had the most loyal people working for us. They wanted to be of service and were never treated like servants.

There was a young boy named Pindar who somehow befriended us, and my parents informally adopted him. He had no parents and did not even know his birthday or how old he was. We guessed he was about my age. They decided July 1 (Canada Day) would be his birthday. For almost 50 years my parents kept in touch with Pindar until they died and would send him money whenever he needed it.

We had several opportunities to travel around the countryside of Nigeria and with Pindar as our interpreter we had many eye-opening experiences. We visited some remote villages where we were the first white people they had seen. We also traveled to the famous Yankari Game Reserve and got our Volkswagen camper stuck in sand on a road at dusk, just as a bunch of vicious wart hogs crossed the road. We cut some branches and put them under the tires and eventually got out. We never forgot it, though. Being stranded when it was getting dark in the wildlands of Nigeria was a harrowing experience.

My parents, brother, and sister slept in the Volkswagen camper. I slept in a tent next to it. The next morning, I woke up first, and as I pulled down the zipper to go outside, I was greeted by a dozen not-so-friendly baboons about 20 yards away just staring at me. Nothing had prepared me for experiences like this.

Additionally, we visited a village where the Fulani tribe lived. Once a year they would conduct the Fulani beatings. This was a ritual where young men coming of age would voluntarily be beaten on their back with a flexible cane. The man who withstood the most lashes got first pick of the eligible women to be married that year. It was a test of honor (and incredible pain) and a completely different courting ritual. It worked for their culture and we were fortunate to witness it. Most Nigerians had to pay a dowry for their wives and our cook, Isa, was amazed when he found out that my Dad married my Mom and did not have to pay for her.

All of this was such a learning experience. I know it has shaped the values I still have today. Watching how the Nigerians were treated by foreigners in their own country was honestly disgusting. My parents were model citizens in how to treat everyone as equals. This is something to this day I try to live up to. I experienced at an early age what it was like being a minority and how that feels, and I also witnessed people being treated like slaves, rather than with dignity. That left a lasting impression on me. The challenges we face today with racial inequality and social injustice are very real and yet could be fixed if everyone respected each other and treated each other as equals. Being kind to others is the easiest thing to do yet seems so hard for many.

When we arrived in Nigeria, we discovered that the school system for expatriates included kindergarten to grade six. After grade six, parents would send their kids to attend boarding school back in their home country. I went to the local school for one semester of grade six. The school was a melting pot consisting of children from Britain, Scotland, Ireland, USA, Hungary, Lebanon, and several different European countries. We were the only Canadians. As I look back on it, we all integrated perfectly. Maybe it was because we were all there from different countries and no one had a "home field" advantage. It was a great experience. For the following year and a half, I was home schooled and tutored.

The great part of going to the local school was the school day ended at 1:00 pm because it was so hot. Each day we would go home for a mid-afternoon nap and then go to the club later in the day to play tennis, golf, or swim. Then we would come home, and Isa would have dinner ready for us. That was the life!

The third year my father worked in Nigeria my parents sent me to a boarding school in England. I was thirteen years old and once again I was a minority – the only Canadian in the school. I was not treated particularly well. I kept being called a "Yankee," which bugged me. I said, "I am not a Yankee, I am Canadian." Their logic was I was from North America so I must be an American, therefore, I was a Yankee. This made no sense to me and one day I challenged their logic and said that since you are all from the British Isles so you might as well be Irish. That led to a fight and the subject never came up again.

Scorton Grammar School, England – 1970 – that is me on the right

The boarding school I attended was called Scorton Grammar School. It was in the tiny village of Scorton in Yorkshire County. It was an all-boys school celebrating its 250th anniversary the year I was there. The main building of the school was a traditional brick building with a clock tower. It had the original wood floors and if the walls could talk, I am sure there would have been some interesting stories. There was a large circular green in the center of the village and legend has it that Robin Hood used to have archery contests on it.

We had a strict dress uniform of grey dress pants, black dress shoes, white or gray dress shirt, a dark green blazer with the school logo on the breast pocket, and a green and gold striped tie. Other than when we had gym class once a week, the uniform was worn all the time – even on weekends!

The food was terrible, and I do not think the menu had been changed in 250 years. It was the same menu every week. We sat at long tables in the dining room with the senior boys at the head of the table and the younger ones, like me, at the other end. The seniors would dish out the food and serve themselves first. The portions seemed to get smaller and smaller as the plates were passed down.

Everything there was based on seniority and it was very disciplined. Sitting at the wrong end of the table also meant doing dishes for the whole table.

We would save up our money and buy fish and chips from the local truck that would come by on Thursday night and park at the gate as we were not allowed out. It would be wrapped in newspaper and we would sneak it into our dorm room and keep it hot on the heaters. I am sure the headmaster had to know we were doing this as the smell in the room was obvious, but he never said a word.

I learned to follow the rules or would get "six of the cane," another foreign concept for me. It meant that if you needed to be punished, the headmaster would whack you across the hand or backside with a cane. Getting hit with the cane sure hurt, but there was a small silver lining. It would warm me up on a cold day.

Although I learned a lot about discipline, I did not learn much about self-discipline. For example, each day I would have six different classes from six different teachers. After our dinner I would have mandatory study hall for 90 minutes in a room with students from all different grades. Some days I would get homework from every teacher and some days I would have none. So, I either would be jamming to get everything done or trying to find something to do during that time. Yet I had to be in that room for 90 minutes no matter what. It certainly could have used my free time to do something productive, instead of aimlessly searching for something to do. The highly structured system did not do much to teach me how to do things on my own initiative, because everything was so regimented.

I lived in a dorm room with eight other guys. There was no central heat, just little heaters under the bunk beds. It was so damp we could put a piece of paper on the wall, and it would stick by itself. The worst thing was, there were two bathtubs to be shared among the 28 guys who were living in the building. There was only enough hot water for two baths in each tub; this meant we each had only one bath a week. Making things even worse, the two tubs were in the open in a big bathroom with the sinks, so there was no privacy at all.

Each year there was a school dance with an all-girls school. That was the only interaction the guys would have with girls in the whole year. Not a great way to learn how to relate to the opposite sex.

The weather in northern England was cold, damp, or rainy most of the time. Overall, it was not a pleasant episode in my life.

One positive experience I did have was making the Yorkshire County Boys Tennis Team. As a member of the team, I got to compete in several tournaments against other counties. The year-end tournament was held on the courts at the famed All England Lawn Tennis and Croquet Club where the Wimbledon Championships are held each year on grass courts. I managed to qualify to play in it. Unfortunately, I had to return to Nigeria a couple of days before the tournament and missed that once-in-a-lifetime opportunity.

At the tender age of 13, I travelled all by myself back to Nigeria for Christmas. That meant getting a bus from Scorton to the city of Darlington, and then boarding a train to travel south to London. I remember sitting and trying to be invisible, as there were numerous "Skinheads" on the train. They were basically gang members with shaved heads who always wore big heavy boots and carried switchblade knives. They struck fear in everyone they crossed. I was terrified.

Once I arrived at the train station in London, I had to take a bus to Heathrow Airport to catch a flight to Amsterdam and then finally make a connecting flight to Kano. There were some weather delays in Amsterdam, which meant having to stay the night in a hotel at the airport courtesy of the airlines. I was assigned a room with another kid about my age in my same situation. Neither of us knew each other. That was a long and scary night. This was well before cell phones, so I had no way to reach my parents to let them know I was delayed. The next morning, I got on a flight for the last leg. What a relief it was to see my parents and I am sure they were relieved to see me, too. How the world has changed. I certainly would not recommend that trip to a 13-year-old going solo today.

One of the perks that came with my Dad's job was each summer CIDA gave all of us a round trip airline ticket to Zurich, Switzerland. My parents would take that ticket and plan a six-week vacation in Europe. The first trip we went to Italy, Greece, Austria, Germany, Spain, and Switzerland. The next summer we saw the Netherlands, Denmark, Sweden, and Norway. It was fun taking a train through the mountains of Norway in July and seeing snow again. On our third and final summer we toured all of England, Wales, Scotland, and Ireland. Then we took the final voyage on the Empress of Canada from England to Montreal, and we were back to normal life again.

We returned to our home in Ste. Anne De Bellevue, and I attended Macdonald High School, on the same campus as Macdonald College, where my parents graduated. As a result of all my experiences and worldly travels, I had a lot more confidence than when I attended elementary school three years before. On the other hand, school was still boring for me and the only thing that inspired me to go to school every day was practice for the many sports teams I played on. Our school had only 800 students and so whatever team you wanted to play on needed you, as long as you had some basic athletic ability.

Macdonald High School – 1974

In my senior year I played on seven teams: football, cross country running, tennis, golf, hockey, volleyball, and track and field. It was not until years later, while attending a personal development course, that I figured out why I was so driven. I was seeking approval from my Dad. He got seven letters in college and I am sure it was no coincidence I played on seven teams in my senior year. Subconsciously, I just had to live up to his expectations. When I finally figured out that I was doing everything in my life for his approval, it was very freeing. Suddenly I felt I could do things because I wanted to and for no other reason.

My senior year in high school was a great one for me. I was voted as the Carnival King at the winter carnival. This was a big deal and got the attention of the girls. The highlight of my year was being selected as Athlete of the Year. My name is still on a big plaque commemorating that achievement in the main hallway of the school. My brother Jim also has his name on the plaque as he was awarded it a few years later. He was a standout basketball player. My coaches, Doug Staniforth and Steve Jackson, were very influential in my developmental years. They both pushed me to excel and taught me to always give it my all, no matter what the circumstance. I may not have been the most talented athlete, but nobody outworked me.

After high school I went to John Abbott College for a year and played varsity football. I did not really enjoy it as I never really fit in with the culture of the team. Most of the guys were big partiers and that was not my scene.

Then I transferred to the University of New Brunswick in Fredericton. I played varsity volleyball and still remember the lessons from my coach, Mel Early. Volleyball has constant momentum shifts and lots of emotional swings. Coach Early always seemed calm under fire, no matter whether we were winning or losing. One day I asked him, "How come you never get too excited?" He replied, "By remaining calm, I can think clearly and always focus on the situation at hand. Getting too emotional doesn't help." Wise words.

I graduated with a Bachelor of Physical Education degree. It trained me to work in a recreational setting rather than being a school-teacher. I also minored in Business. It was in my junior year at university that I started to enjoy long-distance running and that was the start of my love for endurance sports.

The life experiences I had in my early years and the guidance I had from my parents and coaches set me up for success later on. I am forever grateful to them for embracing the risks they took, and by demonstration, showing me, it was okay to take risks. Had they chosen to play it safe, I doubt I would be where I am today.

---♡---

What insights did I gain from this experience?

Taking and embracing risks, as my parents did by going to Nigeria, open up possibilities and learning experiences that I could never imagine. I am so glad they did.

I learned that when I take a risk, I never know the outcome in advance. Often the experience will be quite different from what I expected. I have learned to trust in the process and in my own abilities to deal with any situation that comes up.

All people deserve to be treated as equals.

Being kind to everyone I meet shifts my immediate world and brightens everyone's day around me. The simple act of being kind sets an example for others to follow – just as my parents did for me.

Traveling the world gave me a different perspective on life.

Living in Nigeria and England, as well as traveling throughout Europe and North America gave me new perspectives on how other people live and think. Being exposed to so many different cultures gave me a real appreciation for the life I have.

Regardless of my current situation, I am in total control of the choices I make to determine my future.

I started out in life with low self-confidence. As I set my goals, and then achieved them, my confidence grew and grew. I realize that no matter where I start, it is ultimately the choices I make, and the actions I take, that determine where I finish.

3

IRONMAN: FROM RUNNER
TO TRIATHLETE

1982 - Finishing the Manitoba Marathon in 2:50:41

*"Only those who will risk going too far,
can possibly find out how far one can go."*

– T.S. Eliot, Nobel Prize in Literature.

"Whoever finishes first, we'll call him the 'Iron Man'," Collins said.

The idea for the first IRONMAN Triathlon was born in 1978 on Oahu Island, Hawaii. During the awards ceremony for a running challenge, competitors were arguing about who is more fit: swimmers, runners, or other athletes. In the process, U.S. Navy Commander John Collins remarked that the great Belgian cyclist Eddy Merckx was said to have the highest oxygen uptake ever measured, and therefore cyclists were probably the fittest athletes.

Collins and his wife, Judy, proposed to settle the debate by creating a race combining the three long-distance competitions already existing in Hawaii: the Waikiki Rough Water Swim (2.4 miles), the Around Oahu Bike Race (115 miles – originally a two-day stage race) and the Honolulu Marathon (26.2 miles). Collins suggested that the bike race, by leaving out three miles of its original course, could start at the finish of the ocean swim and end at Aloha Tower, the traditional start of the Honolulu Marathon. As a result, the cycling course was reduced to 112 miles, now the standard bike distance of an IRONMAN triathlon.

Fifteen men participated in the first race and the winner finished in a time of 11 hours, 46 minutes. The next year the race was moved to the Big Island of Hawaii. When ABC's *Wide World of Sports* covered the dramatic footage of Julie Moss crawling across the finish line in February 1982, the event instantly got world-wide recognition and the sport exploded. Later that year, the race was moved to October and has been held annually in October ever since. From its humble beginnings, the IRONMAN has mushroomed into a billion-dollar business with races worldwide. The one in Hawaii is recognized as the World Championship and the grand-daddy of them all.

In February of 1980, I was working at the exclusive Ottawa Athletic Club in Ottawa, Canada. I was an accomplished runner at that time. I had run a few marathons and was running 10-mile runs in under 60 minutes and 10k races in under 34 minutes. I enjoyed racing, but I was so competitive that it bothered me that I would never win a big race. The truth was, I just was not fast enough.

Then one day I was leafing through a Runner's World magazine and my world changed forever. There was a two-page article about the IRONMAN Triathlon World Championship that had just been held in Hawaii. On the two pages there was a photo of a swimmer, a cyclist, and a runner, so you can imagine how little room there was for text to go with the article. I finished reading the article and based on that information alone, I made the decision that I was going to compete in it. I was totally inspired – but was I ever naive!

I knew this was my next challenge, but I really had no idea what I was getting myself into – which was probably a good thing. Had I really known in advance what it would take, I am not sure I would have pressed on. I now had to learn how to combine training for three sports instead of just one and transition from being a runner to a triathlete.

This chapter is a description of some of the obstacles I had to overcome to prepare for race day. More importantly, I describe what I learned about myself from overcoming these enormous obstacles. Make no mistake about it, the IRONMAN is as tough as its reputation, but the training to get there is equally as difficult. In my case, I spent 20 months of relentless training for that one day.

At the time I read that article, I was dating Debbie Prince, who also worked at the Ottawa Athletic Club. She had been one of Canada's top collegiate swimmers and held many provincial records. When I told her of my new goal she said, "Before you go telling everybody about this, let's go to the pool to see if you have the ability to swim 2.4 miles in the ocean."

The club had a small indoor pool about 20 meters long. We went to our respective changing rooms to get into our bathing suits. I was ready first, so I dove into the pool and swam two lengths. I could swim, but it was not pretty. My legs were dragging along the bottom and after two lengths I was exhausted. She came in and said, "Let's see what you've got."

I was only able to swim a couple more lengths. I was swimming front crawl as fast as I could, arms flailing everywhere, and she was on a flutter board beside me just kicking and laughing at me. I could not keep up with her. I realized I had my work cut out for me in this department. I was a fitness instructor, was running sub three-hour marathons, and yet just a few lengths in the pool wiped me out.

She said she would coach me, and our work got started. Our relationship soon developed, and we ended up getting married just two weeks before the IRONMAN and then went to the competition in Hawaii for our honeymoon. Not many brides would put up with that on their honeymoon, but she was as excited about it as I was.

She taught me everything I needed to know about swimming. I was a complete novice. She showed me how to breathe on both sides instead of always breathing to the right. It was so hard for me, but I found it really important when swimming in the ocean, as it helped me swim straighter.

A few months later, I got a job offer to run a pilot employee fitness program for Fitness Canada and we moved to Winnipeg, Manitoba. I joined the Masters' Swim Club that had the use of the Pan Am pool every morning from 6:00 a.m. to 7:00 a.m. It was a great facility with a 50-meter pool and a separate diving pool with all the various platforms. (I never did get up the courage to jump off the 10-meter platform). The pool was purposefully kept cool as it was used for training, not bathing.

Pan Am Pool – Winnipeg, Manitoba
(CTV News)

Imagine this scenario. It is 5:30 a.m. and completely dark. The temperature outside is minus 30 degrees Celsius (-22 degrees Fahrenheit). I am lying in a warm bed with my fiancée beside me. The alarm goes off. Now there is a choice to make. Do I hit the snooze button and enjoy the warmth? Or do I get up, put on three layers of clothes, venture out in the bitter cold, and get into my Honda Civic and hope it starts? That car had vinyl seats that were frozen like blocks of ice in the winter. The three-mile drive to the pool did nothing to get the car warm. Once there, I would strip down into a Speedo bathing suit and jump into cold water and swim for an hour.

Most mornings I made it to the pool – which was more mental toughness training than anything else. I never really learned to enjoy swimming but knew that it was part of the race. As the Navy SEALS say, "I embraced the suck." That discipline has served me well in my later years.

Swimming in a pool is quite different from swimming in the ocean. It is monotonous. Every 50 meters I got to touch the side and take a rest if I wanted. There are lines on the bottom which keep me going straight. Before we left for Hawaii, the longest distance I had ever swum in the pool was two miles. I had serious concerns about the swim portion of the IRONMAN – and that was the first leg of the race.

When we arrived in Hawaii, I had to deal with the challenges of swimming in the ocean. I loved how buoyant I was in the water. I did not have to kick so hard to keep my legs horizontal. But the taste of the salt water took some getting used to and learning to swim straight without the guidance of the lines on the bottom or the edges of the pool or lane ropes was all new to me.

I had to learn how to lift my head straight up to see where I was going without losing momentum while I was swimming. I also had to learn to do this when I was on top of a swell. I found that if I did it when I was at the bottom of a swell, I couldn't see anything, and I just wasted valuable energy.

I loved swimming in the warm waters of Hawaii. Of course, swimming in the ocean also has its risks. One of the competitors was stung by a jelly fish and had to have his eye taped up – yet he still finished the race. Much respect for him. Another competitor got kicked in the ribs in the first 100 yards of the swim and had to withdraw with a cracked rib.

Anytime I swim in the ocean there is always the concern of sharks. This is especially true when I am a mile or more from shore. During the pre-race meeting the day before, the swim coordinator went through all the logistics of the swim.

He talked about seeding yourself at the start with the fastest swimmers at the front, where the sailboat which marked the half-way point was going to be parked, what would happen when you exited the water, how they would have some lifeguards on surf boards in case you got in trouble and reminded us that if you received any help from anyone during the race it was grounds for instant disqualification.

Then to answer the question that was on everyone's mind, but no one was going to ask, he reached down and pushed the play button on his tape deck and the soundtrack from the movie *Jaws* blared over the speakers. The crowd was laughing loudly – but it was a nervous laughter as no macho IRONMAN wanted to admit they were scared stiff of a shark encounter. He then cautioned us that sharks were attracted to thrashing water and bright colors – while they proceeded to hand out our bright orange swim caps. Comforting.

Almost every year at the IRONMAN, dolphins come out of nowhere and swim and play among the lead swimmers, and they also keep the sharks at bay. Unfortunately, dolphins were nowhere to be seen where I was, at the back of the pack.

All the obstacles I had to overcome in the swim section were not even in my consciousness when I decided to enter.

I was even more naive about cycling than I was about swimming. I thought to myself, "I can ride a bike so what's the big deal?"

Ottawa had an extremely active cycling community, and I would often see them riding in large packs on Sundays when the parkway along the beautiful Rideau Canal was closed to traffic. They all wore black shorts and had on these bright-colored wool jerseys which seemed a little odd. Most of them had helmets and cycling gloves but other than that they just seemed like normal people riding a bike. I dusted off my orange 10-speed bike with the Peugeot decal on the down bar. I remember paying $149 for it in high school and thought it was a "bitchin" bike.

Off I went in my short nylon running shorts and singlet, wearing my running shoes and with no helmet or gloves. All seemed to be going well until one cyclist whizzed by me like I was standing still. That really ticked me off, so I downshifted into a lower gear and stood up to go faster. He was gone in a cloud of dust. As a result of my gear change and the extra torque I was applying, the chain fell off.

I was stuck in the middle of nowhere with a greasy chain to put back on. I finally figured it out, but by then my hands were completely black with grease. This really bothered me as I had no real way to clean them, and I had just put fresh white tape on my handlebars. I wiped them as best as I could on the grass and pressed on. After the chain fell off two more times, I was getting to be an expert at putting it back on.

Then a miracle happened. The next time it fell off I was right in front of a high-end bike shop. I had seen this shop before but never paid much attention to it. I wheeled in my bike and asked if they could repair it for me.

The guy said, "Sure. Leave it here and we can get to it in a few days. We are pretty backed up right now."

To which I replied, "Any chance you could do it now? I am in training and I can't wait that long."

He looked at me standing there in my not-so-impressive running gear, with my hands all greasy and asked, "What are you training for?"

"The IRONMAN Triathlon World Championships in Hawaii: part of the event is a 112-mile bike ride.

"Well, where is your bike?"

"You are looking at it!"

The look on his face was priceless. He must have thought I was crazy. He put my chain back on and adjusted it enough so I could get back home. Then he said, "Come back at 4:00 o'clock today and I will take you for a ride on a real bike." I came back at 4:00 p.m. and he fitted me in some cycling shoes and a helmet and put me on a real racing bike. I could not believe the difference. It was like an upgrade from my Honda Civic to a Lamborghini.

I knew then that I needed a new bike. At the time I was making $15,000 a year as a fitness instructor and when he told me the cost of the racing bike I was on, I nearly fell off it. We went back into the shop and he said he had a used Pinarello frame that would work perfectly. He would fit it with all new wheels, tires, gears, components, and everything I would need, including shoes, helmet, and gloves. He would do it all for $1,500. That was 10% of my annual salary.

Me and my Pinarello

That night I swallowed my pride and called my Dad and asked for a loan to buy a bike.

"Sure, how much do you need? A couple of hundred bucks?"

He was just as shocked as I was at the amount but agreed to lend me the money. I paid him $100 a month until it was paid off. That was the first and only time I ever asked to borrow money from him. (As an aside, that same Pinarello today costs more than $12,000.)

Then I needed to learn how to ride that thing. I also needed to learn how to maintain it, fix a flat, keep the chain properly lubed, etc. I knew that if a competitor accepts help from someone in the race they are disqualified. That was the last thing I wanted.

I practiced changing a flat and eventually I was able to do it in under a minute. I could completely take the bike apart and rebuild it. It was one with me. This was another skill I never thought I would need when I was reading the article in Runners World and made the decision to enter.

After a while, I became comfortable riding and decided to test how I would do against other cyclists in a road race. I had never ridden in a pack and was wondering how that would be. I found a race that was 30 kilometers long and figured I could handle that, so I entered. It was a six-kilometer circuit that was completed five times.

I had been in countless running races before, but this was a completely different experience. The race started at 9:00 a.m. and there were about 50 cyclists there. As it got close to 9:00 I made sure I was right at the front of the start line so I could get out in front. For some strange reason none of the other cyclists had the same desire. I was so green. I think someone must have painted "Rookie" on the front of my helmet and forgot to tell me. The joke was on me.

I was all poised at the front with my runner's stopwatch ready to hit the start button. Eventually the starter called everyone to the line and said when you are ready, just go. I took off like a rocket and was pleased about how much of a lead I had quickly built over the pack. It seemed like they could not catch me. After we completed the first lap they were still far behind. I was feeling great about myself.

Here I was just a novice, and I was leading this group of experienced riders. By the third lap I was starting to tire, so I slowed down a bit. Still, they lagged way behind me. Then I could hear them laughing at me. I slowed to almost a crawl and eventually they came up behind me. I felt the loud humming of 50 bikes in a pack as they flew by me. Thank goodness I was able to gain enough speed to tuck in behind the last rider. It was then I experienced the power of drafting. What a difference.

(According to a 1979 study by Chester R. Kyle, you should be able to reduce the drag you experience by up to 44% when riding in a group, assuming you've positioned yourself correctly in the bunch.)

Eventually I maneuvered my way up to the front of the pack. With one lap to go, five of us broke away and left the pack behind. I was a quick study and was tucked in behind the last guy. With about one mile left I made my move and took off on my own and gained a sizeable lead. With 100 yards remaining, I was in the clear except for one rider standing up on his pedals, all hell bent for leather, chasing me down.

I too stood up on my pedals, making a charge for the finish. About 10 yards from the finish my front tire hit a large rock, causing my tire to flip off the rim. Down I went. I literally skidded across the finish line in first place. They disqualified me since I was not "riding" my bike at the end. I think they were just embarrassed that such a "rookie" could beat a group of seasoned riders.

I was a total mess. All cut and bloody. I still have the scars to prove it. It took almost five weeks for my elbow to heal enough so I could swim again.

That was the first and last bike race I ever competed in, but it was worth the experience. Since I knew I could not take advantage of the drafting effect in the IRONMAN, as it was against the rules, there was no sense practicing that style of riding.

When I moved to Winnipeg, I became friends with an attorney named Barry. We would often go for long rides together. He, too, was overly attached to his bike and I learned a lot about cycling from him. He once said to me, "You can touch my wife, but if you ever touch my bike, I'll kill you!" (As an aside he got divorced a while later.) I wonder if his ex-wife touched his bike.

Barry had a cottage on a lake that was exactly 108 miles outside of Winnipeg and we made many rides to it. The road was completely flat for the first 100 miles and if the wind was against us, it made for an exceptionally long ride. About a month before the IRONMAN, I decided to test myself. We left at 1:00 in the afternoon. We got to his place just before dark. I then went for a swim in the lake. The next day, I got up early in the morning and rode home solo and was back before 1:00 pm. I rode 216 miles, with a swim in between, in less than 24 hours.

On the way home I ran into a massive thunderstorm with lightning and torrential rains. There was nowhere to hide on the open prairie so I just kept riding and hoped I would not be struck by lightning. To make matters worse, I had two flat tires to change all by myself in the pouring rain. By the time I got back I was completely spent. I was incredibly pleased, though, with my progress and how far along my cycling skills had come. After that test I felt I could conquer the course in Hawaii. I would soon find out that nothing could prepare me for the hills, the heat, and the lava fields.

Barry and I also did interval training together. We would ride out to a truck weigh station on the Trans-Canada Highway. It was about 20 miles out of the city. We would wait for an 18-wheeler to get weighed and then as it was coming out of the weigh station, we would slip in behind him and sprint as long as we could stay with him. Then we would circle back and wait for the next one. After doing this 10 times, our legs were like noodles and we would ride back into town. I'm not sure that was completely street legal, but I was 25 and foolish and did many things I might not do today.

Unfortunately living in Winnipeg only allowed us to ride for about six months out of the year and we often faced some nasty weather. I just chalked it up to Mental Toughness Training.

At the time I decided to enter the IRONMAN it had only been held three times. Those of us who were crazy enough to enter were the pioneers of the sport. We were inventing our training sessions and trying to figure things out as we went. We were constantly adjusting. There were no instruction manuals. There were no triathlon magazines to read. About six months before the race, I saw that someone published a book about triathlons, but it was not helpful.

Prior to my new triathlon training I was used to running marathons and typically ran about 50 miles a week. My training regimen usually consisted of a 20-mile run on the weekend, followed by a day of rest and a couple of medium runs of about eight miles during the week. The rest of the days I did shorter runs of three to five miles.

Adding the swimming and cycling to my training, I had to make a huge adjustment to my running regimen and cut the mileage way down. I was juggling swimming at least three mornings a week, getting bike rides in regularly during the summer season and doing my best to keep up my running. In the meantime, I was still a fitness instructor and had to lead a couple of fitness classes a day as well. Much to the chagrin of my students in those classes I rarely got my heart rate over 100 beats a minute and they were sweating, out of breath, and trying their best to keep up with me.

The trap for me was to keep myself from doing more and more training. I discovered that I needed more rest and that rest soon became a crucial part of my training.

I kept an incredibly detailed journal to keep everything straight. It held me accountable to myself and allowed me to reflect and adjust on the way. My routine started each morning with taking my resting heart rate when I first woke up. Typically, it was between 50 to 55 beats a minute. If it was higher, it usually meant I needed more rest.

I recorded the weather and the temperature. Winters in Winnipeg are nothing short of brutal. The all-time high for the whole month of January that year was -20 degrees Celsius (-4 degrees Fahrenheit). The sun would come up after 8:00 a.m. and by 4:00 p.m. it was dark. Most nights the temperature would drop below -30. It was like living in a freezer.

I set out my training schedule every Sunday night for the upcoming week based on how the previous week had gone. The key factor for me was no matter what I wrote down as a goal for that day, I pushed myself to finish it. Some days, the goal might be to ride 100 miles, some days it was to run three miles and some days the goal was just rest and stretching.

After several months of writing something down and then doing it, my mind became convinced into believing that no matter what I wrote down I could do. This would prove especially critical on the day of the IRONMAN, as my brain just went into automatic pilot. Instead of saying I was going to run three miles and then doing it, that day's goal was to swim 2.4 miles, ride 112 miles and then run 26 miles, 385 yards. To my brain it was all the same.

Of course, if I had wavered from doing what I said I was going to do, my brain would constantly be wondering if I could actually do what I set out to do that day. As a result, I would be less than powerful. I didn't want that to happen. Over time, and a lot of repetition of keeping my word, my confidence level got stronger and stronger. That is where my true power came from – keeping my word, no matter what.

Running in Winnipeg posed its own challenges. There was no indoor running track, so it was either run outside or not at all. I got the gear I needed. Lifa long underwear to wick sweat from my body, another layer or two of cotton clothes to absorb the additional sweat, with a Gore-Tex wind suit to cut the ever-present wind. Often, I wore two hats, caked my face with Vaseline to prevent frost bite and on the coldest days I would wear a surgical mask. I also had specially designed runner's mitts made of Gore-Tex that had no thumb so I could clench my fist inside and keep all fingers and my thumb warm.

I learned to NEVER run starting with the wind, because I would quickly get sweaty and then when I turned around and ran into the wind, the effective temperature drop with the wind chill could easily be 20 degrees. I only made that mistake once. The snow in Winnipeg was also different than in Ottawa where I lived when I started training. It was never slushy, always hard packed, and often slippery. It was so cold that the foam in the heel of my running shoes would freeze and become hard. If I slipped ever so slightly and clipped my ankle with my shoe it felt like someone hit it with a hammer.

The summers posed another challenge. It got hot and humid, and the mosquitos were as big as four-engine bombers. They were relentless and could not be outrun, as much as I tried.

During my 20-month training in preparation for the IRONMAN, I was always looking for ways to test myself, as I knew the race would be the hardest thing I had ever attempted. I wanted to be as ready as I could. There were no triathlon competitions of any distance anywhere near Winnipeg. Almost nobody had even heard of the IRONMAN and I was the only competitor in the province of Manitoba to go to Hawaii. So, I organized a triathlon on my own. I called it the

TINMAN and it was half the distance of the IRONMAN. About 20 competitors showed up and it was a great learning experience.

Another unexpected obstacle was that the race organizers decided to switch the date of the IRONMAN from the usual date in February to October. Their logic was that many competitors like me were training in cold climates and moving it to October made sense. The only problem was that my two-year training program was focused on competing in February. Now, half-way through my preparation I had to decide to either cut my training short by four months or wait another year.

I took the risk and decided to go earlier, even though I wished I had more time to train.

This whole experience was ground-breaking for me, and completely different when I was competing on sports teams throughout my life. This was 100% individual effort, and I had no coach to guide me.

By the time I got to Hawaii, I felt as prepared as I could possibly be. Now it was time to see who would win – me, or the course.

What insights did I gain from this experience?

I had no idea what I was getting myself into – and yet somehow, I adapted along the way.

The amount of information I had when I decided to take on the IRONMAN was less than 1/100 of what I needed to know. In fact, had I really known what I was getting into, I likely would not have started. Despite this lack of understanding, I had faith in my ability to adapt.

I learned the importance of keeping track of my daily progress in a journal.

Doing so kept me accountable to myself and allowed me to adjust based on accurate statistics. This is a practice I transferred into my business life and continue to this day.

I am capable of doing way more than I think I can.

Training for the IRONMAN is a test of both physical and mental limitations. By setting daily goals and completing each one – no matter what – I strengthened my body. More importantly, I trained my mind to believe that no matter what I said I was going to do that day, I could do it.

4

RACE DAY

Here I am, finishing the swim – IRONMAN – October 9, 1982

"Until you face your fears, you don't move to the other side, where you find your power."

– Mark Allen, Six-Time IRONMAN
Triathlon World Champion

I t's 4:00 a.m. and the alarm just went off. I was already awake, waiting for it to mark the start of my big day. The date is October 9, 1982. I am in Kailua-Kona, on the Big Island of Hawaii. Today is the day. The biggest athletic challenge of my life. The IRONMAN Triathlon World Championships.

I am about to compete with almost 900 finely-tuned athletes from all over the world. I am so excited, nervous, apprehensive, and down-right scared that I can barely stand it. Time to get up and do some carbo-loading. I need to store as much fuel as I can, as it will be a long day. It's dark outside and there are just three hours until the start of the race.

After eating and getting dressed, I sit quietly to stretch, meditate, and visualize how the day is going to unfold. In my mind's eye I see myself successfully completing the 2.4-mile swim in the Pacific Ocean, riding 112 miles through the hot lava fields of the Big Island, and then facing the ultimate runner's test, the 26.2-mile marathon – all in fewer than 12 hours. I had no misconceptions about winning. Finishing was the main objective, and if I could do it under my time goal, I would be ecstatic.

I do my best to eliminate any negative thoughts, but this is my first time doing this and who knows what will occur today. I know that to get through this day I need to stay positive.

An hour before start time I make my way down to the beach. The energy is electric. The world's finest-conditioned athletes are crowded on the small beach, nervously waiting. Each one seems to be looking inward, not sure what to expect. We are so close our shoulders are rubbing together.

We are seeded in the water based on our expected finish time for the swim. The field includes Olympic and NCAA Champion swimmers. They are in the front. I am near the back of the pack.

I anxiously gaze out into the ocean, looking for the sailboat with bright orange sails. It is moored 1.2 miles straight out from shore. That is the turning point. It is like a speck bobbing on the horizon. It turned out to be quite a large boat when I got to swim around it, but from the beach I could barely see it. Before arriving in Hawaii, just ten days earlier, I had never swum in the ocean, and I had never swum 2.4 miles in one shot. Naturally, this fact had me on edge.

Time seems to be standing still as I watch the large digital time clock count down the minutes and seconds until the start of the competition. It is taking forever. I can't get my heart to slow down. I had been in countless races; and other athletic competitions before, but never experienced the level of these feelings. It has been said that fear and excitement have the same body sensation. Today I have a double dose of each!

Finally, the gun goes off. It is like turning on a blender in the water. Arms and legs are flailing everywhere. Just trying to get some space of my own to swim was a challenge. Unlike when I was training in the pool, there were no lines on the bottom of the ocean to follow. Should I follow the person in front of me? Who knows if they can swim straight? I decide to follow my own path and every twenty strokes look up to see those orange sails and make a correction if necessary. Given these conditions, I am sure I will swim way more than 2.4 miles today!

The intense and chaotic start of a triathlon

Eventually everything calms down and I have some space of my own. The water is crystal clear, and I can easily see 40 feet below. The colors of the fish are brilliant – vibrant yellow, electric blue, with a variety of stripes. Even though I am in this competitive state I cannot ignore the beauty beneath me – it is almost hypnotic – but I have to remain focused on the task at hand. This is way better than the Pan Am swimming pool I am used to training in while living in Winnipeg, Canada.

After a while I settle into a rhythm. Mostly I am swimming front-crawl and I switch to breast-stroke when I need to rest a bit. The boat looms larger and larger and finally I arrive, swim around it, and head back to shore. The people on the boat give me some applause and words of encouragement. That helps me to forge ahead.

Already my lips are swollen from the salt water, which surprises me. I am so grateful that my new Barracuda goggles are working fine and not allowing any water in. I can't imagine the sting in my eyes the salt would cause.

By the time I reach the turnaround point, some of the world-class swimmers have already completed the swim and are on their bikes. I am not too worried about how far ahead of me they are as I know I will see many of them on the bike course and during the marathon. I know I have to stay within myself and not be concerned about others. This is totally an individual race.

After one hour and 46 minutes, I finally get to shore and exit up the concrete ramp. Just getting out of the water is a huge accomplishment and I am so elated to get that event out of the way. There are people cheering everywhere and my adrenaline kicks up a notch. I am in 646th place at that point. Some competitors have already dropped out.

The organizers have the logistics down to a science. Someone is reading off my number which is written on my arm with a big black marker, and then shouts my number to the next person, who has my prescription sunglasses ready for me to put on. Then I run through a portable overhead shower to rinse off some of the salt water.

A volunteer escorts me to a tent where I have my numbered bag ready with my spandex cycling suit, cycling shoes, helmet, and gloves. I feel so honored to put it on and represent my country and my sponsor, Canadian Pacific Airlines, (CP Air). They generously donated two first class tickets for the trip to Hawaii. My employer, Canada Safeway, had given me $500 and I was on my own for all my other expenses. The top of my cycling suit is white with bright orange trim, which are CP Air's corporate colors. The shoulders have the distinctive Maple Leaf of Canada and the Safeway logo prominently displayed. The bottoms are black – a color that did not work too well in the heat. I have created this outfit, which was more like a uniform to me, just for today and it gives me a huge boost, just to put it on.

I quickly change and run out to find my bike, a hand-crafted Pinarello, made in Italy. It is painted flat black with the Pinarello logo in bright yellow. This custom-made bicycle is a work of art. There are millions of dollars of these human-powered machines, all lined up in rows at the start of the bike race. I wish I could take the time to admire them all, but the clock does not stop during the transitions, so there is no time to rest.

I get on my bike, put my feet in the toe-clips and head off through the massive crowds lining the road, and cheering us on. The noise is deafening, and I am absolutely loving it.

Getting energy from the crowd at the start of the bike course

Just half a mile down the road I hit the first hill, which is super steep. That is so tough. All the blood is still in my upper body from the swim and now I have to force it down into my legs to get them to work. After the tough climb, I make a left turn and head out on the King Kamehameha Highway for 56 miles to the turnaround point, which is the sleepy town of Hawi (pronounced Haw-vee).

Soon the crowds are thinning out to nothing and I begin the journey through the hills and heat of the lava fields. This portion of the race is an environment like no other. It looks like a moonscape. There are no trees for miles. The asphalt road is jet black. The temperature is already 90 degrees by that point, with high humidity and trade winds whipping off the ocean. It is not even 9:00 a.m. yet. I know I am in for a hot day. Then add in the hills and it quickly becomes the most challenging 112 miles I have ever attempted. This race is a lot different from the "flat-earth" training I am used to in Winnipeg.

The lonely bike course at the IRONMAN.
The turn-around at Hawi is up the hill in the distance

Unlike normal bike races where there is a large pack and you can draft behind another rider, this is an individual event – I have to stay at least two bike lengths apart or risk disqualification.

This enforced separation has two consequences. I can't take advantage of the drafting effect, making the ride considerably harder. It also means there is no one to talk to. This arduous stretch is a daunting ride to do solo. Keeping my mind focused and positive for 112 miles is torturous. I often trained with other cyclists in Canada, but none of them made the trip with me so I am completely on my own in Hawaii.

I start to assess how I am doing. I am elated that the swim is out of the way. Now I just need to focus on the ride and not have my mind drift.

The bike course has aid stations every five miles where we switch out water bottles. I can't get enough water and often am drinking two, 16-ounce water bottles every five miles. Never once do I have to stop to pee. At the aid stations are all the bananas I can eat, along with sandwiches with guava jam – a local favorite. I am also carrying a

53

small canvas bag strapped to my handlebars with my own concoction of trail mix, dried papaya, and pineapple.

Knowing how many calories I am going to burn today creates a constant effort of eating and drinking, while still trying to breathe. Endurance events are such a delicate balance of exertion while trying to stay relaxed, hydrated, and fueled. I lost count of how many bananas I ate and was happy I had learned earlier how to peel a banana with just one hand while riding my bike.

Feeling good at this point in the race

As I get closer to the turn-around point at Hawi, I encounter a relentless seven-mile climb. I switch into first gear and pound away on my pedals. It seems to take forever. There is a small crowd at the turn-around encouraging us. With my legs feeling like jelly, making that U-turn is so hard just to stay balanced. I am exhausted, but grateful to be retracing the route back to Kona. Now for the fun – the seven-mile descent! I don't even have to turn my pedals. I am hanging on for dear life and my triceps are aching by the time I get to the bottom. Every now and then a gust of wind off the ocean hits me from the side, almost blowing me over. Fortunately, there is not much traffic on the course, as it is closed except for security and TV crews.

To keep my mind focused, I just keep looking at the person in front of me to track them down, and then pass them. That seems to work for a while, until I get to about mile 80. Suddenly there is no one in sight. As I gaze down the road, I can see the heat mirage coming off the black pavement. The 25-mile-an-hour trade winds are creating a whistle in my helmet. My feet are getting swollen, and I am sure the temperature six inches off the black pavement has to be well over 120 degrees. I have black-leather cycling shoes with small holes in them for ventilation. Again, the wrong choice of color in this heat.

My mind starts to wander – I am so exhausted I am almost hallucinating. I still have more than 30 miles to ride and when that is done the marathon is looming. I have already run six marathons before the IRONMAN, so I know full well what the run entails. A marathon on its own is more than enough of a challenge, but with a "warm-up" of a 2.4-mile swim and 112-mile bike I seriously begin to doubt if I can finish. I am already spent!

Fortunately, my years of visualizing pay off. I start acknowledging the successes of the day so far and just keep focusing on the short targets in front of me and not looking too far ahead. Finally, a rider then comes into my vision. I track him down and blow past him. From that point on I never look back. I just keep passing people.

As I approach the town of Kona, the crowds are gathered again and that gets my adrenaline flowing. After 6 hours and 38 minutes of sitting on a tiny and uncomfortable bike seat I finally get to the next staging area. What a relief. I finish the bike section, moving from 646th place to 456th place.

Another volunteer takes my bike and guides me into the ballroom of a hotel where once again I change – this time into my running clothes and running shoes. I sit on a hard wooden bench putting on my shoes thinking how comfortable the bench is compared to my bike seat. I sit there for a minute gathering myself to get ready for the run.

My feet are so swollen from the bike ride and the salt water, I can barely get my shoes on. As my shoes are now too small, my toes keep banging the front of my shoes during the run. After finishing the IRONMAN, I ended up with six toenails going completely black and eventually falling off. Fortunately, they all grew back several months later.

Once out the door another steep hill faces me. Not the way I want to start a marathon. Now my challenge is to get my legs to switch from going in a circular motion to a forward and back running motion.

The run is my strength and so I resume targeting those in front of me and chasing them down. I am proud to say that not one person passed me on the run, and I had the 10th fastest run time among all IRONMAN competitors that year.

The way the run course is set up, I can see the finish line about eight miles into the run before heading back out to the highway for most of the run. As I near that eight-mile spot, a deafening cheer erupts from the crowd. Dave Scott, the winner that year, has just crossed the finish line in a time of 9 hours and 8 minutes – an incredible feat of athleticism.

For a brief moment, that realization is deflating and gets me down. I still have 18.2 more miles to go, and the race is already over for many of the elite participants. Then I snap out of it and remind myself of my personal goal of finishing in fewer than 12 hours. So far, I am right on track.

The run course takes me back out to the desolate King Kamehameha Highway where the bike course finished up and there are still very tired cyclists coming in.

On the run section there are aid stations every mile with water and oranges. The high energy GU gel packs that every runner uses today had not been invented yet.

I face those same hills and the relentless head wind that I had endured previously on the bike course.

This is my first time to Hawaii. I am startled that when the sun goes down, it seems to go from sunlight to complete darkness in about 10 minutes. The sun sets at 6:00 p.m. It is now pitch black. There are no lights on the road and without warning it starts to rain. It feels so good because it is cooling me off, but now I cannot see, as my glasses are all foggy.

This is an out-and-back course, so I have to be aware of the runners coming toward me. How many more unexpected obstacles can this race put in front of me? The IRONMAN is sure living up to its reputation of being the most iconic test of endurance in the world.

Once I get to mile 20, I start to feel like I can actually finish this thing. But then doubt creeps in again. Experienced marathon runners know full well that mile 20 can feel like the halfway mark of the 26.2-mile race. This is not the time to take the last 6.2 miles lightly. Anything can happen in those last 6 miles, 385 yards!

I recall how just four months earlier I ran the Manitoba Marathon in Winnipeg, with the goal of qualifying for the esteemed Boston Marathon. At that time, for my age group, I had to run it in under 2 hours and 50 minutes. I was on pace to beat that time right up until the very last mile. I completely ran out of gas and ran the last mile 41 seconds slower than the others and finished in 2:50:41. I am determined not to make the same mistake again and remain focused on the runner in front of me.

When I get to one mile from the end of the race, I know I am going to finish. I go completely crazy. I run the whole of the last mile with my hands above my head, yelling and screaming at the top of my lungs. I never felt such elation in my entire life. I can see the finish line in front of me with the big digital clock. As I run under it, I look up and it reads 11 hours, 55 minutes, and 37 seconds. Goal achieved. I forever remember that one moment in time.

With the Finish Line in sight

I later found out I had finished in 181st place, meaning I had passed almost 300 runners along the way to end up in the top 20% in the world.

As I crossed the finish line a volunteer placed my Finisher's Medal in my hand, and another draped a flower lei around my neck. The Finisher's Medal, with its iron hue, was heavy. It's a treasure worthy of the effort to get it. As I clutched my medal I was overcome with emotion and I must admit I shed a tear or two. I had just finished and earned the title of IRONMAN!

IRONMAN Finisher's Medal

Then I was led to another area where they had a bunch of massage therapists who volunteered to give your legs a quick rub down to get some of the lactic acid out of them.

Just walking a few hundred feet after the race was incredibly difficult. It is amazing how my mind supports me to get to the desired goal and then once there, it shuts off and my body is left to figure it out on its own.

That day was a pivotal one in my life, and I still gather strength from it regularly. When the going gets tough I just reflect on that day and say to myself, "This can't be too hard compared to that 12-hour day!"

Many people have asked me why I did it. I joke, saying, "It was for the Finisher's T Shirt" – which is long gone. Really it was for the sense of accomplishment. It's no different from climbers who conquer Mount Everest. There is no prize – just the incredible feeling of accomplishment.

While in Hawaii I went into the store of the official jeweler for the IRONMAN, looking for some sort of memento. I had him design a ring for me, which is centered around the logo cut into a gold band. For me it is like my Superman ring. Every time the going gets tough

I just look down at my ring and it puts everything in perspective. Pretty much every day since October 9, 1982 has been an easy day.

What did I learn from all of this – aside from gaining an incredible amount of confidence in myself?

Something I never expected! I occasionally watch the event on TV. I watch it like most spectators, and I am in complete awe. I look at the terrain, the pain on the faces and listen to the commentators describing what they are going through. Each time I watch it, I marvel at what I am watching, and I honestly ask myself, "How do they do it?"

That seems like such an odd question given that I have already done it! The truth is I do not know how they do it. Looking back, I can say with 100% certainty I still do NOT know how I did it – and I have done it!

I was back in Kona a few years ago on vacation and drove most of the bike course in a car. As I drove, I was shaking my head, still wondering, *How did I do this?*

Why is this question so important to me? It makes me realize that knowing the answers in advance of setting a goal is completely irrelevant.

———————— ♡ ————————

What insights did I gain from this experience?

I don't have to have all the answers before I take on a big goal.

The key takeaway for me is that even after I have accomplished something as big as the IRONMAN, I still do not know how I did it. I continue to set big goals for myself and push my limits. Now I have stopped looking for the answers in advance and just take the first step forward and make many adjustments along the way. The journey is never a straight line from A to B. Sooner or later I know I will get there if I never quit. Knowing this truth deep in my bones frees me up to go after things I would never think possible.

I no longer ask the question of myself, "How am I going to do this?"

My truth is, I may never know — even after I have achieved my goal! Now I simply ask myself a better question, "Is this something I really want to do and if so, am I committed to seeing it through to completion?" If the answer is yes, then I begin, knowing that I have the tenacity and resources to achieve absolutely anything I set my mind to.

The journey is as valuable as the finish line.

The exuberance and excitement of crossing the finish line was a fleeting moment in time. Hardly worth the enormous effort. In addition to finishing the race, my secondary goal was to cross that finish line in fewer than 12 hours, which I also achieved. I have learned to embrace the journey and not just focus on the result. The IRONMAN opened many doors for me and still lives in my soul almost 40 years later. The many rewards that have come are far more valuable and long-lasting than simply focusing on that singular moment of crossing the finish line.

5

MY GREATEST FEAR

The Podium
(Artist: Ben Humbert)

"The way you overcome shyness is to become so wrapped up in something that you forget to be afraid."

– Lady Bird Johnson,
First Lady of the United States, 1963-69

The fear of public speaking is the number one phobia ahead of death, spiders, or heights. The National Institute of Mental Health reports that public speaking anxiety, or glossophobia, affects about 73% of the population. The underlying fear is judgment, or negative evaluation by others. Public speaking anxiety is considered a social-anxiety disorder.

I shared that fear – deep in my bones. I was terrified of being at the front of the room and freezing up. Not knowing what to say, and the words just would not come out. People staring at me with all their judgments.

All through high school and university I did everything humanly possible to avoid being put in that situation. Whenever there was a choice of doing a presentation or handing in a written assignment, I would always choose the written assignment. If there was a presentation that had to be made, I always tried to see if it could be a group presentation and I would be at the back of the group (one of the advantages of being tall).

After I completed the IRONMAN Triathlon in 1982, I was hired by London Life in Ottawa to sell life insurance. Right at the beginning I had to go through an intense three-week training program at their home office with 30 other candidates. During that time, we did a lot of role-playing with a partner. I was okay with that, but toward the end of the program we had to do a role-play in front of the whole class. We had to pretend our partner was a live client and go through a 20-minute memorized sales pitch. That was terrifying.

Now there was no escaping this. If I wanted to keep my job, I had to do it. I did my best to just focus on my partner and ignore the rest of the class, but it did not go well. My nerves got the best of me and a couple of times I lost track of where I was in the presentation. I got through it, though, graduated from the program, and did very well with one-on-one sales.

I realized the fear of not being able to speak to even a small group was going to cost me in terms of lost sales and missed opportunities for advancement. I decided I needed to deal with this fear head-on but had no idea how.

Soon after I returned to Ottawa, I met a client who had just completed the Dale Carnegie Training program. She loved it. I asked more about it and found it was a 12-week program to teach you how to speak in public. I knew that was what I needed – but then I had to find the courage to enroll.

It took several days but I finally got the guts to call for information. I was used to making sales calls for appointments, but making this call meant I was committing to face my fear of speaking in public. I was told there was a class starting that night and there was one spot left. The next class did not start for 12 weeks. I realized I had to start that night – if I let this opportunity go by, I might never have the courage to take it on again. I decided to jump in – even with all my fears. I knew I had to deal with this sooner or later.

I went to the class and like everyone else, I was very apprehensive of what was going to occur. There were about 20 people in the class from all walks of life. Most were older than I. The instructor was great and did his best to put everyone at ease. To break the ice, he led us through an exercise where we introduced ourselves to one another so we would get to know each other – something really straight forward. He sent us to the front of the room in groups of four.

Looking back, it was an extremely simple exercise. We just had to say our name, how old we were, where we were born and what we did for a living. He even had a big table at the front of the room we could lean against or even sit on. He did everything he could to make us comfortable.

I was in the last group, so of course the waiting only added to the tension. I found my breathing was shallow and my palms were sweaty. Finally, it was time for our group to go to the front of the room. I looked to my right at the man beside me. To say he was nervous would be a huge understatement. He was sweating profusely. His whole forehead was covered in sweat, his glasses were all fogged up and there was a bead of sweat dripping off the end of his nose. I really felt for him. Somehow, he got through it, as we all did.

Over the course of the program, we all slowly gained confidence and before I knew it, I was looking forward to going to the class.

Each week was different. At first, we just had a dialogue with the instructor. One of us would be at the front of the room and he would be walking around among the audience asking us questions. This allowed us to avoid being paralyzed by thinking ahead. We would just answer the questions he gave us, but we were at the front of the room. Gradually we felt more comfortable.

Then he taught us how to engage with each person in the room. Each person in the audience would stand, and the goal for the person at the front was to induce each person to sit down. Once you had made eye contact with them and they really felt it then they would sit down. This was a great exercise to make sure you were speaking to everyone in your audience. We learned how to work a podium, and how to command a whole stage.

Another week we had to do a demonstration using a prop. I demonstrated how to change a flat tire on my bicycle in 60 seconds.

Soon we were required to prepare a 60-second speech and then deliver it. The feedback from the instructor and participant was always positive. By the end of it I was getting a high from being on stage. What a transformation that was.

In the last class we each had to give a two-minute speech about something we had experienced in life where we learned a big lesson. I decided to share about competing in the IRONMAN. The talk was very well received. I was so elated I had kicked this fear that had been holding me back in life from so many opportunities. I wanted more of this feeling – it was a rush! I truly felt I had a message to share and now felt good about doing so. Now I just needed an audience.

The very next day after graduating from the class, I was going for a run at lunch with one of my buddies. He was the president of one of the big banks in Ottawa. Halfway through our run I made another declaration that altered the course of my life.

In between breaths on our run, I announced to my friend, "Gary, I just finished taking the Dale Carnegie Course and have decided to become a professional speaker." He was kind of shocked and replied, "That's wonderful. What made you decide to do this, and what will you be speaking about?" I told him I wanted to share my experience of competing in the IRONMAN and how I have applied the training principles I learned in sports to business.

What he said next caught me off guard and opened my path to become a professional speaker. He shared that he was a member of the Ottawa Rotary Club that meets every Friday for lunch and they always have a guest speaker. He was sure they would like to hear my message and said he would put me in touch with the Program Chairman. What a vote of confidence that gave me.

We finished our run, showered, and I went back to the office. I was not there 15 minutes before I got a call from the Rotary Club Program Chairman inviting me to speak to the club. He said their speaker for the following Friday had to postpone and asked if I could fill in. I said, "Sure – I would be happy to."

I had no idea in that moment what I was committing to. I then asked where it was held and how many people would be there. He told me they meet at noon in the Grand Ballroom of the Chateau Laurier (one of Canada's landmark Canadian Pacific Hotels) and there are usually about 150 people in attendance. I had 20 minutes to share my message.

Immediately the terror set in. This was a whole new ballgame. But I had made the commitment – there was no backing out now.

CP Hotels are known for their grandeur and this ballroom was no exception. I walked in and was awestruck by its beauty. The ceilings had to be 40 feet high with huge chandeliers. Natural light was streaming in from huge dome windows that almost reached to the ceiling. In the distance you could see the Parliament buildings of our nation's capital and the Ottawa River. What a sight.

**Site of my first public speaking engagement –
The Chateau Laurier, Ottawa, Canada, 1984**

Now I had to calm my nerves. Talk about jumping into the deep end. My last talk was just a week earlier at the graduation of the Dale Carnegie course and was only two minutes long in front of 20 people. They were all going through a speaking course together and were a very compassionate audience. Now I was going to be addressing 150 people who I did not know, from the podium on stage, in a huge ballroom. Yikes. What had I got myself into? I was riding solo in a strange new environment. There were no training wheels available.

Lunch was served first, and then the Rotary Chairman conducted his business. I hardly ate anything and was just focused on breathing and trying to relax. Then I was introduced and had to climb the stairs up to the stage. I had never used a microphone so that was another new experience. I remember I sounded different. After that, I do not remember too many details of the actual talk. It was an out-of-body experience. Yet somehow, I got through it. I received a nice ovation at the end, and I felt extremely validated. I did it. I conquered my fear.

I have since learned that it is never a good idea to address a group right after they have eaten a big lunch as they tend to want to nod off. I somehow managed to get through the 20 minutes and everyone was still awake (although there was one elderly gentleman in the front row who was starting to drift off toward the end.)

I got some surprisingly good feedback which I did not expect after my rookie experience. A week later I had a call from another Rotary Club nearby and was invited to address its meeting. The news was spreading. Then it was the Kiwanis Club, the Optimists Club and so on. Pretty soon I was speaking almost every week somewhere.

I was always a hero in the eyes of the poor Program Chairman whose job it was to secure 52 speakers a year – all speaking for free. They loved me for filling a spot, and the audience really seemed to connect with my message. Business owners and salespeople left with some real tools they could start applying immediately. What a great platform it was for me to practice speaking, gain my confidence, and hone my skills. I highly recommend it to anyone who wants to start a speaking career.

When I told my Life Insurance Manager what I was doing he was supportive, as it did not conflict with my work and allowed me to meet new people in an extremely positive light. Although this was not my motivation, it was great for sales. His brother managed an insurance office in Toronto, and I was invited to speak there. It was so well received that I was soon speaking in many of the London Life Offices in Ontario.

One day I had a call from the head of the Ontario Life Underwriters Association. He invited me to be the keynote speaker at their annual convention. I had attended the convention the year before and instantly recognized what an honor that was; I accepted immediately. All this happened in less than a year after graduating from Dale Carnegie.

As soon as I hung up the phone, I remembered what a huge audience attended those meetings – at least 2,000 of the best life-insurance agents in the province. Instantly the fear came up again. This was a whole new territory. I did my best to calm down and tried rationalizing that I had given this talk numerous times and I could handle it. But something about the size of the audience and the massive stage, spotlights, etc. was gripping me. I also feared that maybe I would not live up to the expectations of being the Keynote Speaker.

The night before, I was pacing in my hotel room and I became paralyzed. I wondered what I would do if I forgot my speech part way through. I knew my talk like the back of my hand but still this fear kept coming up. I decided to make some cue cards just in case. I got about 20 index cards and wrote one key word in big letters on each card. That would be the cue for the next section. I put them all in order and rehearsed one last time in my mind. I was ready.

Early next morning I went to the theater with the other speakers, and we were given a tour. We started backstage and it was immense. The curtains were 30-feet high and there were cables everywhere. I peered out to where the audience would be seated. It was gorgeous with three tiers and the opera balconies on each side. The chairs were plush red velvet.

We then walked on stage to do a sound check. This was my first experience standing on a massive stage with a spotlight in my eye. It was blinding and prevented me from seeing the crowd. Maybe that would turn out to be a good thing. But normally when I speak to an audience, I feed off their energy and realized this was going to be a challenge. I would not be able to see them.

I was on last, so I took a seat in the audience and enjoyed the presentations leading up to my keynote presentation. Just before I was to go on, I went backstage to get ready. I was a nervous wreck but kept telling myself that once I got started, I would be fine. I was glad I was wearing a dark suit as it was already wringing wet. I focused on taking deep breaths and I reminded myself of how far I had come from that first night at the Dale Carnegie Course. I kept saying to myself, "*You got this!*"

The organizers informed me they were short one microphone and we had to share one so when the speaker came off the stage, he would give me his while they were introducing me. They were old-school lavalier microphones that were suspended on a cord that hung around our neck.

The last speaker came off stage and there I was with my cue cards in hand ready to go. He kind of fumbled the transfer and I had to reach out to grab the microphone. In doing so, I dropped my cue cards on the floor.

I was horrified. My heart was racing, and my eyes were watering. I only had about 10 seconds left until the end of my introduction.

I knew this because I had written the introduction the emcee was reading. I quickly stooped down, gathered up the cards and miraculously they seemed to be in order. Not the way I had envisioned getting prepared to go on stage.

I took a deep breath and strode out on stage. I got the cue off the first card and off I went. I looked down at the next card, got my cue and kept going. Then I looked at the third cue card. It was the cue for my closing comments. For a split second I panicked. Fortunately, I remembered what the next segment in my talk was, so I took the cue cards and put them in my breast pocket.

That was the last time I ever used cue cards again. The talk was a big success, and I received a standing ovation. As much as I was fearful of this big stage, I found it was an incredible high and I wanted more.

Until then, all my talks were done with no financial compensation. I declared to myself it was time to start charging. I visualized that it would be a cool experience to fly all over the country giving talks. That would be validation that I was a real professional speaker. It is so amazing how quickly the universe supports you when you get clear on your goal, write it down, and make a declaration.

The very next week I was giving a talk at a luncheon. When I finished, I was seated at a round table and started a conversation with the lady next to me. She was the head of a sales organization that had offices all across Canada. She loved my presentation and wanted me to deliver it to their sales force. Turned out that in a few months they were having their annual sales meetings in five cities across the country. She said, "I know this is a big ask, but would you be willing to deliver your talk in the five cities? It would be a commitment of almost 10 days, and they could only pay you $10,000." How quickly that goal manifested itself. I made arrangements with my manager to take the time off work, and also got the blessing from my wife.

I started on the east coast in Halifax, and along with the heads of the company, we kept going west. The next day was in Montreal, then on to Toronto, Calgary, and finally Vancouver. It sounds glamourous and they put me up in fancy hotels, but after the second night they all looked the same. I was giving the same talk to different audiences and soon it felt monotonous. A five-city tour in 10 days is wearing on the body and the soul. I checked that box on the goal sheet and was glad I did not invest any more attention to travelling around the country.

I have had many wonderful experiences speaking – and some harrowing experiences. I remember filling in for a good friend of mine at a sales conference in Pittsburgh. He was sick and called me the day before. They were paying $5,000 for a one-hour talk, so I jumped on a plane to take his place. I met the organizers that night. Our talks were completely different, and the audience was expecting someone else. I kind of felt like being a warmup band at a rock concert. I hoped the audience would be polite and listen, but deep down I knew what they really wanted to hear was the main act.

I went to bed that night to get some rest and be ready for my talk the next evening. I woke up with the worst case of laryngitis. I could barely get out a whisper. I rested my voice all day, gargled with salt water and by the evening I could still barely talk but figured with a good microphone I could pull it off.

They gave me a proper microphone that I attached to the lapel on my suit jacket. I was all set – except for when I stood on stage to start there was no sound. Absolutely nothing. The silence was deafening. Turns out they forgot to change the battery and it went dead right at the start. They eventually got it right and I was able to get through it.

Another learning experience – always do a sound check before going on stage.

Over time I started teaching my own seminars and rarely travelled again. I preferred to have people come to me to hear me speak in my environment where I could control the conditions. It was a lot safer that way.

I started my own seminar company and regularly gave seminars that would be two full days in length. These seminars were primarily business and marketing courses, but I always mixed in personal development. I discovered that the biggest thing holding people back from being successful in business was rarely a lack of information.

Rather it was something in their personal life holding them back (like the fear of public speaking had been holding me back).

My seminar business soon evolved to a successful coaching business where I really got to know my clients. They were paying me for personalizing business and marketing plans for their company, which I did. However, the biggest impact was working on their personal goals and helping them break through their fears, while holding them accountable. It was the accountability factor that made the biggest difference in their results.

Never in my wildest dreams could I have envisioned that outcome while introducing myself the first night of The Dale Carnegie class. I remember that introduction like it was yesterday (it was 37 years ago). I was terrified – now I love being on stage. I love teaching and watching lightbulbs go on in my student's heads.

Just recently I had a call from a student who took my marketing course more than 25 years ago. He thanked me for what a profound influence I had been in his life. I have watched many of my students' businesses grow exponentially and it is so fulfilling that I was able to have an impact on their lives.

I cannot help but think of how different my life would be today if I did not have the courage to enroll in the Dale Carnegie class. Likely I would still be avoiding speaking in public. I would be living my life in a shadow. All the information I wanted to share would be kept to myself. All the thousands of people I have touched in my talks and seminars would have been robbed from that experience – all because of my fear of speaking in public.

I wish that the skill of Public Speaking had been a mandatory class in my high school so I could have dealt with that fear earlier on in life.

I am so proud I conquered that fear when I did and am grateful to be able to contribute to the lives of others.

———————— ♡ ————————

What Insights did I gain from this experience?

The ability to speak in public is a learned skill – it is not something we are born with.

Conquering my fear of speaking in public opened doors for me I never thought were possible.

I learned that by facing my fears head-on, I can accomplish anything I want.

The longer I put off doing something because of my fear, the bigger the fear gets. I have learned that it is better to tackle something head-on, right away, rather than letting it fester. Something I thought I could never do, turned out to be a big rush of adrenaline. Fear can be turned into excitement.

Fear never really goes away completely.

That was evident by how I felt when I got invited to speak at bigger events. With practice, fear can be managed and even become a joyful experience.

6
CREATING A LEGACY
FOR UNCLE EDDIE

Start of the New Brunswick Heart Marathon, April 15, 1979

"If you are losing faith in human nature,
go out and watch a marathon."

– Kathrine Switzer,
first woman to run the Boston Marathon, 1967

Getting the call from my parents that my Great-Uncle, Eddie Mulligan had suddenly died of a heart attack was an extremely traumatic experience for me. I was away from home, in my junior year at the University of New Brunswick in Fredericton, and this was the first time I had experienced anyone close to me dying. I was 500 miles from my family, all alone, and did not have anyone to share my grief with. I didn't know how to express my sadness, or even sort out what I was feeling.

Uncle Eddie was a wonderful human being. He did not have a mean bone in his body and was always jovial. He had recently retired and was in his late 70's when he died. He spent many years as a used-car salesman and once you met him it was obvious why he was so well suited for that. He was the kind of man who just immediately put a smile on your face and made you feel at ease.

In his later years he was the chauffeur for the Mayor of Ottawa, the capital of Canada, and a city of nearly one million people. He was so beloved, that the mayor donated his home on Island Park Drive to Uncle Eddie and his wife Aunt Mina. Uncle Eddie always had a twinkle in his eye and rosy red cheeks.

Me and Uncle Eddie, 1959

I remember many weekends when the two of them would make the drive to Montreal from Ottawa. My Dad would always have a Rye and Ginger with lots of ice waiting for him. Then Eddie would settle in my Dad's big brown leather recliner and typically have a cat nap. They often traveled with us when we would go camping; they would stay in a nearby hotel and join us for meals at the campground. He would always joke with my Mother about all the space she was taking up in the cooler with milk, when it could be used for the ginger ale that would go with his rye whiskey.

Soon after Uncle Eddie died, I felt inspired to do something to honor his memory. Since he died of a heart attack, I vowed to raise money for the New Brunswick Heart Foundation. My best friend, Garth Cochrane, and I had been doing a fair amount of running, along with his dog, a German Shorthaired Pointer named Sam. We decided to run from the campus of the University of New Brunswick to the Mactaquac Dam, 18 miles away. We got pledges from as many people as we could and set the date for the run on April 19, 1978. We had never run more than 10 miles before, so this was a big challenge for us.

The day of our run was cold, windy, and rainy, but the experience was exhilarating. My roommate, John Blair, drove his car behind us to make sure we were okay and had water for us when we needed it. There was little fanfare, and only a few people to cheer us on at the end. The city newspaper, The Daily Gleaner, came out and took a photo of the three of us and soon Sam was nicknamed "Sam the Wonder Dog."

**With Garth Cochrane and "Sam the Wonder Dog"
at the start of the Mactquac Run**

Garth, Sam, and me at the finish

That was my first real experience with long-distance running, and I was hooked. There was something about the solitude that was so peaceful. Getting into a rhythm, listening to the sounds of my breathing, and feeling my heart-beat put me in a calming trance. I soon experienced what was called the "Runner's High." It was certainly a lot different than banging helmets when I played college football.

Looking back, it is hard to believe I ran that distance in Converse basketball shoes and knee-high socks. Soon after that run, I bought my first pair of real running shoes – one of the first models that Nike made with the waffle design on the sole.

In my senior year of university, one of my professors challenged everyone in our Physical Education Practicum class to take on a project that was fitness-related and would make a difference in the community. Since I had completed the Mactaquac Run, I had been wanting to run a marathon and I soon realized there were no big marathons being held in Fredericton, so I decided to organize one and take that on as my project.

To make the event especially meaningful, I resolved to use it as a fund-raising tool for the New Brunswick Heart Foundation. My project was approved by my professor, but she explained I would need permission to use the foundation's name and logo. I contacted the Heart Foundation and informed them of my project. They wanted to hear my proposal and invited me to make a presentation at their monthly Board of Directors meeting, held in Saint John, about an hour's drive away.

My roommate John generously offered to drive me, as I didn't have a car. This was my first experience attending a Board of Directors Meeting and I was nervous. Speaking to a group like that was a huge stretch for me, but I was extremely passionate about what I wanted to accomplish. I made the false assumption they would be equally as excited as I was to have the marathon named after them, not to mention it would raise much-needed money for the foundation.

When I walked into the room, I was greeted by eight members. The president was in his late forties and the rest of the board members were at least 70 or older. Based on how they appeared there was no sign of any runners, except for me.

I made my presentation and immediately following, I was met with an objection I had not anticipated. Their biggest concern was that someone might die of a heart attack during the race. They were afraid that would not be a good look for the Heart Foundation. I was studying Physical Education at university and although I could certainly not guarantee a completely safe outcome, the risks were minimal, as most marathoners are very fit. After an hour or so of conversation I finally got their blessing. The director was all in.

On the drive back to school, I realized that I wasn't going to get much help from the members of the board based on their less-than-overwhelming enthusiasm, so I started my list of things to do to organize a marathon from scratch. I had no idea what I was doing and had never even competed in one. I figured that participating in a marathon as soon as I could, should be my first step.

I found a small marathon organized by the YMCA and decided to take part in it. Only problem was, it was in three weeks and I did not have time to adequately train for such a long race. It was a small event with only about 30 entrants. We ran a shorter circuit of five miles that we kept repeating, with the last mile and 385 yards on the track that surrounded the YMCA. Once again, my friend Garth and Sam the Wonder Dog decided to enter. We were young and fit and somehow managed to complete it in a time of 3 hours and 20 minutes.

The last several miles were gruesome, but Sam was loving it. When we finished, Sam was getting everyone's attention. Lots of treats and hugs for the dog. He was definitely the star attraction. I will never forget hobbling into the shower at the YMCA after the race. I shampooed my hair and by the time I finished, my legs were so tight I could not bend down to pick up my shampoo bottle. I just left it there.

I had now experienced my first marathon. I learned a lot just by going through the registration process. I also saw how they set up aid stations, how the start and finish lines were arranged, how the timing was done and how the awards ceremony was conducted. This was a far cry from the large marathons that are held today, but it was a start.

I started my checklist of things to do. It was soon a long list. The first thing on the agenda was to determine the route and measure and map out the course. I did not have many resources to draw on. The most accurate measuring method I had was a car, and I had to borrow one.

My friend had a beat-up, old, dark green Volkswagen Beetle. We used it to determine the distance as accurately as we could. A true marathon measures 26 miles, 385 yards. I was hoping we were pretty close. Fortunately, his odometer was still working but that was about the only thing that did. We were driving the course one cold winter day to get the measurement, when all of a sudden, we started to encounter freezing rain. His defroster did not work and neither did his wipers.

Soon we could barely see out the windshield. I told him to roll down his window so he could look out. That did not work either. So, I rolled down mine and put my head out the window so I could guide him. Eventually we had to pull over to scrape the windshield and wait for the freezing rain to stop. The joys of being a starving student! As I look back, I am amazed we survived that day.

Once we had the course mapped out, I went to the Fredericton Police Department to get their approval, as it was all being run on city roads. Part of it was even on the two-lane Trans-Canada Highway, Canada's major east-west thoroughfare. The police were incredibly supportive and helpful. A couple of weeks before the event I received a letter from one of the big churches in town, objecting to the start line being so close to their church. They were afraid it would interfere with their Sunday-morning service. We made the adjustment by moving the start line 300 yards, and everyone was happy.

We established the date and time and then I started promoting the event. This was long before we enjoyed the use of personal computers, so just creating a flyer was hard. I went to the graphics department at the university, and they helped me out. Together we designed a simple flyer with a registration form at the bottom. I started posting it all around town and mailed some to YMCA branches in other cities in New Brunswick. I did not have the luxury of social media to promote the event, and I had a bare-bones budget of $400 from the Heart Foundation for expenses and marketing costs.

I researched how to create a press release and sent it to the local newspapers and radio stations. The main disc jockey on the biggest station in town grabbed hold of it and did a phenomenal job promoting our marathon. He had an immensely popular morning show with a huge following. Someone close to him had died of a heart attack and he was excited to support the event to raise money for the Heart Foundation. He gave the event tons of exposure and since it was just him sharing about it on air, I did not have to pay for any radio ads.

With him being a radio personality, I had no idea what he looked like. He just had a very deep and distinctive voice. He was a very gentle man with a great spirit. When I finally met him, I was shocked. He had to weigh at least 300 pounds, and he wore a big black cowboy hat. He drove a huge pickup truck with double rear wheels. The fact that he was promoting a marathon seemed odd to me as he certainly would not be participating. I never questioned his motives and was so grateful for his help. I never expected support from him, and he turned out to be a big factor in making the event successful.

I will never forget that when we were close to the race date, he put on a big push for the event on his radio program and asked if he could call me to do a live radio interview. This was another first for me. We set it up so he would call the phone in our dorm. The phone was located in a tiny phone booth in the hallway. This was all happening during finals week at school. Between studying and organizing the race I got run down and lost my voice.

I did not know what to do as I could not get more than a whisper out of my mouth but certainly did not want to pass on that great opportunity. My roommate John, who had been living through all the planning with me, stepped up and said, "Let me do the interview for you. I know everything there is to know and since it is radio no one will know it is not you." The two of us crammed into that tiny phone booth and John acted like he was me. Somehow, we pulled it off. To this day, the DJ does not know it was not me on the radio.

Then came the challenge of the T-shirt design. Some runners would enter races just to get the T-shirt – so that was a big deal and the shirt had to be perfect. Without a computer I had to design it all myself by hand. I got out a plain piece of paper and started to create it. I began with a protractor to draw a large circle. That was to symbolize the circle of life. Inside the circle, I drew a heart with a runner superimposed on it. Since I didn't have a computer to do any of the lettering I went to the bookstore and bought one of those templates for tracing letters and numbers and used it to write *First Annual New Brunswick Heart Marathon, April 15, 1979* around the circle.

I then found a T-shirt company that offered to silk-screen the shirts for free as a donation to the Heart Foundation. I bought white T-shirts with red trim on the collar and sleeves, and I made the logo all red. I was pretty excited about what I had created from nothing.

Then a similar process was done to create the Certificate of Completion. Once they were printed, I had a friend personalize each one by hand-writing the participants name with a black calligraphy pen on the certificate. It turned out to be a work of art, one that any marathoner would be proud to frame and display.

In order to drive up more participation and more donations to the Heart Foundation, I decided to add a 10K race at the same time. That proved to be a smart decision, as there were not many marathoners in the province to draw from. Soon registrations started to flow in – and each day I looked forward to opening my mailbox to find entry forms coming in from all over the province. My parents, and brother and sister, came all the way from Montreal to run the 10K. My brother even brought some of his friends who were great runners. By race day we had 32 registered for the marathon and well over 100 for the 10K.

My parents finishing the 10K run

I'm grateful that many of my fellow classmates and friends from my dorm volunteered to help out that day. Standing at the start line with a bull horn welcoming everyone and seeing the huge crowd of runners and spectators was a proud moment. The New Brunswick Heart Marathon banner was hung across the road at the start line. A police car was at the front with lights flashing, ready to escort everyone as we headed out of town. They had intersections blocked off for us and ensured everyone was safe. The race went off without a hitch and the Heart Foundation could breathe a sigh of relief that no one had a heart attack.

My only regret was that I could not personally run in the event as I had to stay focused on making sure everything went as planned.

Four and a half hours later, the last of the marathoners came in while we were in the middle of the post-race dinner, celebration, and awards ceremony. The event was a total success and raised more than $10,000 for the Heart Foundation. I was thrilled with the outcome. At the same time, I was exhausted. I discovered organizing an event like that without a staff or committee was a real challenge. All decisions were made by me and, with the exception of race day, I did the lion's share of the work.

**The Awards Ceremony with Vince Galbraith, Director,
New Brunswick Heart Foundation**

I received an A+ for my grade in that course and still managed a B+ average for my other courses with all that was going on during finals week. Having put all that work into it, I wanted to make sure that this race would continue on long after I left the university. My professor assured me it would, and the following year another student took it on and carried the torch. I am elated to say that although the sponsors and the charities the race supports change each year, it has been running continuously ever since – still going strong 41 years later.

Although I am not running any more, fitness is still a huge part of my life. I am so grateful knowing that each year thousands of participants are still flocking to Fredericton each May to compete in the marathon. I am humbled and honored to have laid the foundation for that event and know it continues to make a difference for thousands each year. I am so proud to have started a legacy that continues on in my absence.

R.I.P. Eddie Mulligan - *your memory lives on.*

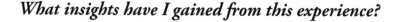

What insights have I gained from this experience?

A determined person can make a difference in the world just by making the decision to do so, and then following through with action.

By making up my mind that I wanted to create an extraordinary event that would raise thousands of dollars for a good cause, I set the wheels in motion for something absolutely wonderful. By following through with dogged determination, careful planning, and creatively employing the limited resources around me, I was able to make something much bigger than I ever imagined.

When I do something for the good of others it completely shifts the dynamics of everything. It makes me more accountable and allows for others to participate in the mission.

As I was creating this event to honor my Uncle Eddie, I drew on the inspiration he provided me. At times it was as if he were watching over me, giving me strength and guidance. Uncle Eddie inspired many others who never even met him.

When I set a big goal, the assistance I receive often comes from the most unexpected sources.

I have learned to trust that whenever I am up to something big, the universe will provide whatever I need, whenever I need it. It is not linear or logical. A perfect example is having the DJ showing up out of nowhere to help promote a marathon.

A project worth doing is worth doing well. Looking back, I had absolutely no experience in what I was trying to accomplish but I decided to throw myself into it and do it as well as I could. Energy and enthusiasm can overcome any lack of experience.

The inspired, untiring effort I put into this project ensured it would be a success, despite the fact that I knew very little about what needed to be done when I started. My enthusiasm and positive outlook carried the day, even when I was confronted with seemingly insurmountable obstacles. My Dad taught me to have this unbeatable, never-say-die perspective early on in life, and I carry his lesson with me always.

7

THE MILLIONAIRE CLUB

One Million Dollars

*"Before you can become a millionaire, you must learn
to think like one. You must learn how to motivate
yourself to counter fear with courage."*

– Thomas J. Stanley, author of
The Millionaire Next Door

He stood up at the front of the seminar room holding up a one-dollar bill and asked the question, "If I could guarantee to give you this dollar bill in five years, how much would you pay for it today?

People started shouting numbers like 10 cents, 25 cents, 5 cents and so on. Then someone said, "I will give you a penny." Raymond said, "SOLD!"

Then he asked, "How many dollar bills do you want to buy at a penny today?" Miraculously, and right on cue, that person said, "I'll take a million." Raymond once again said, "SOLD! That will be $10,000 – thank you."

That was the birth of the Raymond Aaron Millionaire Club. I will get more into that later, but first let me share how I met Raymond Aaron.

It was 1988, and I was in my fifth year of selling life insurance. I had been quite successful, qualifying for membership in the Million Dollar Round Table each year. Membership was reserved for the top 3% of agents worldwide from all companies. It was quite a prestigious club to belong to – but I was never satisfied.

During my career selling life insurance I kept searching for ways to better myself and to improve how I conducted my business. One thing I did early on was to not see people at their homes at night. I found that was the least productive time to sell. People were tired and I had no control of whether they had a bad day or not, so I switched my hours and made myself available in my office from 6:00 a.m. to 6:00 p.m. (no one ever took the 6:00 a.m. appointment). By seeing people in my office, it was on my terms and I was viewed much more as a professional. I was only 26 years old when I started and could barely balance my check book, so anything I could do to improve my posturing was a good thing.

I also started taking personal-development courses. I took the Dale Carnegie course and a time management course. Then I enrolled in The Forum. It was the first time it was offered, and it was a spinoff from the Erhard Seminars Training (EST) that was created and led by Werner Erhard – a personal-development guru from San Francisco. It was a challenging seminar to get through over two weekends, where we really went deep into what makes us tick and what was holding us back in life. By the end of it I had many personal transformations and "ah-ha" moments.

I started to learn why I was living my life the way I was. It was not easy being vulnerable to myself and others. After the course, I stopped living for others and started living for myself. I could not get enough of this personal development idea, and for almost three years I was involved in their programs and was working my way up to becoming a seminar leader.

After four years in the life-insurance business, I had built a solid client base and I had gone more than 200 weeks of having at least one sale a week. Most of my sales would net about a $1,000 commission. I was making a decent living but always seemed to have more expenses than income. One day I decided to switch things up and figured if I sold to millionaires and multi-millionaires, I could make infinitely more money for the same amount of effort. This one decision was a huge turning point in my life!

I decided to spend Monday to Thursday doing what I called my "Bread and Butter" business to insure I kept my momentum and income stable. I dedicated Fridays to going after the "Big Fish." There was only one problem, and it was a BIG one – I did NOT know any millionaires. At the young age of 31, I was not living in the circles millionaires do and was not one myself either.

It was only a week after I made that declaration that I was in my office late in the afternoon, reading the newspaper searching for prospects, and saw this huge ad that read, "Self-Made Millionaire Will Teach You How to Make Millions in Real Estate – Free Seminar tonight at 7:00 p.m. at the Westin Hotel."

The word "millionaire" jumped right off the page (since that was on my radar). Here was my chance to meet a millionaire - and it was free! How could I lose? I went to my buddy's office next door and invited him to come along. He looked at the ad and said, "That will be a big scam." He had no interest in going.

Having nothing to lose, I went on my own. The seminar was being led by Raymond Aaron. He was the most captivating speaker I had ever heard, and he completely shifted my perception about real estate. I had bought two homes in my lifetime and the last one I had to sell as it cost too much to hang on to it. That was a painful experience, and I was renting at the time. Naturally, I was somewhat jaded when it came to real estate.

Raymond Aaron sharing his words of wisdom

Raymond completely shattered everyone's beliefs about the concept of "Buy Low and Sell High" and taught us how almost everyone "Buys High and Hopes to Sell Higher." At the end of the free seminar, Raymond offered his weekend seminar that was starting that Saturday. The cost was $395.

I went home that night and told my wife Debbie I wanted to take the course. She asked how much it was, and I told her it was $395. She was hesitant. "We don't have that kind of money to be wasting on a foolish seminar. Plus, we do not have the money to buy any real estate, so why even go?"

I tried to explain to her that was precisely the reason for going – so we could become wealthy by investing in real estate. Making commissions was never going to get us there. She was having nothing to do with it. We had a huge disagreement, and I went to bed fuming. I just tossed and turned. Then about 3:30 in the morning (when I seem to get my best ideas) I woke up and thought, *Here is a millionaire that I could approach to sell a big policy and if I was successful, I would have the money to take the course.*

I lay awake trying to figure out how I could approach him. At the time, the company I was with was offering a unique whole-life insurance policy. After seven years of paying premiums the policy generated enough dividends to pay the premiums for the rest of your life. It cost more than term insurance but at the end of seven years you owned it and the death benefit would eventually be paid to your estate. Here was my ticket. I could offer it to him as an investment property.

I got dressed in my best suit and was in my office by 7:30. I guessed Raymond's age to be about 40 and ran the printouts on a $1,000,000 policy for him. The annual premium was $26,000 (which is what I would earn in commissions from the sale of this policy over two years!)

I figured Raymond would likely be staying at the hotel where the seminar was held. I decided to wait until 8:00 a.m. before calling him. I had the hotel clerk ring his room and I figured if he sounded like he was sleeping I would just hang up and call later. Fortunately, he was wide awake. I introduced myself (but left off the part I was with London Life). I took a moment to acknowledge Raymond for the great job he did the night before leading the seminar. I then told him I had a unique property that was worth a million dollars that I wanted to show him. I told him it had an unusual payment plan for it. You just pay 2.6% ($26,000) a year for seven years and then you own it. No more payments. That got his attention.

He asked if he could see it. I told him I had the plans in my briefcase and would be happy to show them to him. He said, "I am free all day until my evening seminar." My office was a short five-minute walk to the hotel so by 8:30 a.m. I was in his room (only five hours from when I conceived of the idea). And no coincidence, I'm sure – it was a Friday – the day I had dedicated to selling to Millionaires!

We hit it off right away. He was a runner and when he saw my IRONMAN ring he was impressed. After getting to know each other a bit he asked to see the "property." I pulled out the spread sheet for a $1,000,000 life insurance policy and explained how it worked.

As I had experienced a shift in my thinking on real estate the night before, he had a similar shift in thinking about life insurance. He decided right away this was a good investment, and he completed an application – and I just made my biggest sale ever! One of the things I love about working with successful entrepreneurs is that they make decisions quickly.

I then went back to Debbie and we agreed that since I had earned such a big commission it made sense to take the course. I immediately enrolled in Raymond's seminar for that weekend.

I went back to the office to begin processing the application and about 10:30 my buddy from next door came strolling in. He was in a foul mood as he had been at someone's home the night before until after 9:30 at night and did not make a sale. He asked how the seminar was and I just showed him the application and said his decision not to go was a big mistake. Just like the classic scene in the movie *Pretty Woman* where Julia Roberts goes back into the shop where a salesgirl refused to serve her the day before. With her arms full of shopping bags from another store, Julia asked the same salesgirl if she worked on commission and said, "Big Mistake, BIG Mistake!"

I attended Raymond's seminar that weekend and it was a life-altering experience. Raymond broke down all the myths about real estate I had gathered over the years and then gave us a step-buy-step process to invest in real estate. I began putting into practice what he taught and within a couple of months bought a town home for us to live in. I had a friend put up the down payment of $15,000, I put in a dollar and we moved in. It was not our dream home, but it was a start to get my foot back into the real estate market. Using this joint venture strategy, I was able to acquire shares in 24 investment properties in just a few years.

A few months later, Raymond was back in Ottawa with his weekend course. I surprised him by going to the Free Seminar where I knew he would be selling his course. I had taken a picture of our townhome and had it framed with a one-dollar bill below it. I put a caption on it that read, "Thank you Raymond, for Teaching Me How to Buy this Home with this Dollar." He was moved and I am sure it helped his sales that night.

After the seminar, he wanted to talk to me and asked for my help. I stuck around and he said he was having a challenge with his seminars. It seemed a good percentage of people would take his course and then share with their spouse, parents, or their buddies at work the next day that they were going to start investing in real estate. Instantly they were shot down in flames by family and friends who hadn't attended the seminar, and the whole course was wasted.

He was trying to figure out a way to get those people back on track and thought that perhaps doing a "Super Seminar" would do it. I listened to his dilemma and asked more questions. I reminded him that his course worked – I was living proof of that. After listening to Raymond, it appeared to me that most of his graduates wanted to put his seminar to use but faced similar challenges. Either they had low self-esteem, no support structure, negative people around them, negative thinking in their head or a combination of all the above. They were good people who just needed some guidance outside of the sound real estate investment advice he was giving

No weekend "Super Seminar" would ever fix that. I knew from the past several years of taking personal-development seminars that it was the people themselves who needed help. It was NOT a lack of information that was keeping them stuck – they were getting in their own way.

I asked Raymond how long it would take for a person to go from zero to a millionaire if they followed his principles. He quickly answered, "Five years." "Okay let me think about it and I'll get back to you," I shot right back.

That Thursday night I went to bed and at 2:00 a.m., I once again awoke. This time I had a vision of the solution to Raymond's dilemma. It would be called The Millionaire Club and it would be a five-year program designed to teach people how to think, behave and look like a millionaire in every aspect of their life. We would personally mentor them for five years.

We were one of the first ever to offer a coaching program like this. We would offer a variety of seminars on everything from time management, how to dress for success, goal-setting, relationship building, speaking powerfully, living with integrity, positive affirmations, being accountable, and much more.

I lay awake for two hours and created this whole program in my head. I called Raymond early in the morning and told him I needed to meet with him right away while everything was fresh, as I had not written anything down. I went back to his hotel and laid out the whole plan. He loved it and we decided to go into business together!

We decided to charge $10,000 for the initiation fee and would have 100 people in the program. Then we would charge a monthly fee for the ongoing seminars. If you do the math, 100 people at $10,000 each is one million dollars.

Raymond was doing a free seminar that night to sell his weekend course and just before the break he said he had a huge announcement to make. He then introduced the Millionaire Club concept. Again, the beauty of working with people like Raymond is they do not take forever to analyze something to death. If it feels right, they go for it. This concept was less than a day old, yet he wanted to test the market to get their reaction.

As described at the start of this story, Raymond stood up at the front of the seminar room holding up a one dollar bill and asked the question, "If I could guarantee to give you this dollar bill in five years, how much would you pay for it today? After he got the answer he was looking for, and ultimately everyone's attention he then briefly described the program (remember the concept was still less than a day old.)

He said we are not taking applications yet, but we are creating an interest list. If you think this might be for you, go to the back of the room on the break and add your name and contact info to the Interest List. No sooner had he finished that sentence when about 2/3 of the people jumped out of their seats and ran to the back of the room. Some were jumping over chairs to get there first. I caught Raymond's eye and we looked at each other and knew right then we had a winner.

We met a couple of times the next week to work out details. He contacted his friend, Bob Proctor, a master in the personal-development business, and Bob gave us his input. Within a week, we had the foundation of the program set. Raymond would sell it to his existing client base of 10,000 graduates, and his staff would run the logistics. My role was to create the program, organize the seminars and bring in the best experts available on each subject. We agreed that the whole first year would have nothing to do with real estate and would focus entirely on personal development.

The following week I walked into my manager's office and told him I was resigning to pursue this new venture. He thought I was out of my mind and I was taking a huge risk. He said, "There is no guarantee this will work." To which I answered, "I am working on 100% commission here. What guarantees can you offer me?"

Starting The Millionaire Club meant moving from Ottawa to Toronto and starting a completely new life. I was so excited. What a wild ride the next few years were. I got to hear some of the best speakers in the world give their seminars in Toronto.

Some of the notable ones were:

Mark Victor Hansen and Jack Canfield, co-authors of the *Chicken Soup for the Soul* series of books which is now a publishing empire. They taught us how to ask for what we want, and how to love ourselves.

Martin Rutte, a pioneer of Spirituality in the Workplace and now author of *Project Heaven on Earth*, delivered his course called The Success Factor. He taught us to be accountable for our own lives.

Stewart Emery taught us personal integrity. Stewart is a legend in the personal-development world and one of the only people on the planet who can say that he personally trained Werner Erhard, founder of EST.

Bob Proctor, one of Canada's most beloved personal-development leaders and author of *You Were Born Rich* shifted our perspective on money.

We had many full-day workshops on a variety of topics. I remember one where we gave people complete makeovers. We brought in hairstylists and wardrobe experts and by the end of the day you hardly recognized some of the participants. One young man named Nicholas, was about 25 and a self-proclaimed "rebel with a rock band" – and was going nowhere fast. He had long blond hair down to his shoulders. His hat was on backwards and he always wore these grubby overalls, old high-top running shoes and a ratty, long-sleeved shirt. He went into the back, had his hair cut short and came out in a $1,200 Armani suit. People did not even recognize him. By improving his grooming and wardrobe, his true brilliance shone through and his odds of attracting an investor skyrocketed that day. Within a year, he owned 12 properties.

My own life changed forever, as I became friends with all these speakers who had years and years of experience and were all millionaires themselves. While I appreciated my office colleague who I described earlier, this experience helped change my perspective and, along with that, it changed who I spent my time with. Now I was in the constant presence of millionaires who had already achieved success. I had the ability to interact and be mentored by them. I saved myself years of making mistakes and my whole way of thinking changed.

The Millionaire Club was wildly successful, and the speakers loved coming to Toronto to interact with this group. They had never had the opportunity to present to a group of people that had spent $10,000 each to hear them. Most seminars started with a standing ovation before they even started. The participants were thirsty for knowledge and these leaders delivered, big time!

After six months we decided to open the enrollment again, and then again, a year later. We eventually had 300 people in the program.

I was sitting in one of the seminars led by Mark Victor Hansen and he challenged us to be more tomorrow than we were yesterday and to really stretch ourselves. He suggested we take the focus off ourselves and put it out there in the world. Even though I was responsible for coaching all the people in The Millionaire Club I still felt room to grow and stretch.

I was inspired to do something about Canada's national debt. It was astonishing to me that each year the government would spend more money than it brought in. Yet they tricked Canadians into thinking they were doing great because they were reducing the deficit. When I first heard that statement, I thought they were working on reducing the debt. When I realized they were just reducing the amount they were overspending each year, I was disgusted and angry. So, I decided to do something about it. I formed a nonprofit organization called Bank on Canada. The name was a play on words of Bank of Canada, which is Canada's National Bank. Our mission was to have the country be debt-free by December 31, 1999 at noon. That gave us just over 10 years to accomplish the mission.

I set up an office, hired an assistant, and got to work. I sent out a national press release to let media outlets know what we were up to. We were on the map, as it immediately got the attention of the media. What was most interesting was the media were more focused on the time I had given to accomplish the goal, rather than the actual goal itself. They kept asking why I had chosen December 31, 1999 at noon. I simply replied that it made us accountable. They were invited to call me at noon on December 31, 1999, and ask a simple question, "Is the Government of Canada debt free?" Without a specific date and time that goal would never be measured. It started to get traction and people started sending in donations. I had them write the checks to The Government of Canada.

Here I was, a young 33-year-old with absolutely no political experience and yet I was raising money for our federal government. Several months later I shared the experience with Mark Victor Hansen when he was back giving another seminar. He was so impressed he brought me up on stage and introduced me as the next Prime Minister of Canada. That took me by complete surprise. I had never thought of myself in that role and have to admit I gave it some serious consideration.

A few weeks later I gathered up all the checks we had collected. Most were small checks between $10 and $100 but they totaled several thousand dollars. I wrote a personal letter to Canada's Prime Minister, Brian Mulroney. I explained what we were doing and let him know that we were there to support him, and this money was not to be used for any programs, but rather to be applied to paying down the national debt.

Much to my surprise I received a personal letter from him stating that although he very much appreciated the support and gesture, he had to return the checks as there was no mechanism in place to pay down the debt. I appreciated his integrity of returning the money but was completely dumbfounded. I suddenly realized what a huge establishment I was up against. I returned all the checks to the donors and ended that program. Any desire I had of going into politics was gone.

About a year into The Millionaire Club, we started to notice our participants falling into three distinct groups.

There were the chronic over-achievers. They ate this stuff up. Within a year or so, their lives had completely changed. They were so busy being successful they really did not need the program anymore and they kind of self-graduated, and only came to select events. They got more than their money's worth.

Then there was the group that realized that "In order for things to change, first I must change." When they looked in the mirror, they did not like what they saw, but were also unwilling to do anything about it. Some just dropped out – one lady after the first event forfeited her $10,000. Some people would rather be right than rich.

Then there was the third group who I call the "seminar junkies." These are the ones who figured that by just attending a seminar their lives would change. Really nice people, but subconsciously committed to staying stuck. They go from seminar to seminar, searching for the magic answer and not realizing the answer was within themselves.

Each group benefitted in different ways, and Raymond and I were always challenged to provide something for everyone. It was an incredible study of human behavior. Not everyone graduated to become a millionaire, but every person's life was impacted in a positive way.

It's amazing to think the incredible journey I just described began with me not having $395 to take a seminar. Because of that, I was forced to use my creativity and courage to make that first call to Raymond and ask him to buy a million-dollar life-insurance policy.

It is incredible how, when I decide to do something, how quickly the universe will make it available to me. I just need to be clear on my intention, be open to receive and then be ready to take the action when the gift comes.

What insights did I gain from this experience?

When I make a commitment to something new, I can easily attract new people to turn that commitment into reality.

The energy that was generated from The Millionaire Club became like a magnet, attracting incredible people to us.

Things move at light speed when I am fully committed.

How quickly I met Raymond Aaron, my first millionaire client after deciding to sell insurance to millionaires was beyond my wildest expectations. The speed at which The Millionaire Club came into being, from just a thought in my head at 2:00 am, was head spinning.

Generating money can be extraordinarily simple.

It took only three presentation meetings to enroll our first 100 people into the program. At $10,000 each that was $1,000,000.

Surrounding myself with those who have already accomplished what I am looking to do accelerates my growth faster than any method I know.

Being in the presence of, and learning from, so many successful people catapulted my growth. I was like a sponge absorbing lifetimes of experience in a concentrated timeframe.

8

HONORING COMMITMENTS

Boeing 737 Airplane
(BBC News)

"People who are interested in doing something will do it when it's convenient. People who are committed will do it no matter what."

– Bob Proctor, best-selling author,
You Were Born Rich

At 8:00 p.m. I was standing at the front of the class I was leading and there was a loud knock on the door. In comes a man, 30 minutes late. I told him class had already started and he needed to leave and could come back next week. He left.

Two minutes later he came barging back in, stormed to the front of the room, and got right in my face. He was a big burly man, and his nostrils were flaring. He was visibly upset. I was intimidated by him but managed to stand my ground. I am sure it looked like the classic confrontation between a baseball umpire and manager. If there had been dirt on the ground, you can be sure he would have kicked it on my shoes. He proceeded to tell me that he had to cut a meeting short to be on time and he might lose a million-dollar real-estate deal as a result. I reminded him he was still late, and it was totally his choice to cut his meeting short. We had already started, and he needed to leave. He left cursing and swearing. It was not pretty.

Waiting for someone who is late for a scheduled meeting is frustrating. I feel disrespected that my valuable time might be wasted. All of us probably feel the same – it's a common reaction.

During my time with The Millionaire Club, I had the privilege to create a six-month leadership program. I called it the Unlimited Potential (or UP) Program. I was inspired to design and lead a program where people had the opportunity to stretch themselves and maximize their potential. I was super excited to take it on. The first topic we dealt with was time commitments.

I taught the program in both Ottawa and Toronto and had about 50 people in each program. I would travel back and forth between cities and would lead a two-hour evening session once a week.

At the time I was only 32 years old and the fact that I was leading a group of 100 men and women, most were older than I, was both inspiring and somewhat terrifying at the same time. There was no manual for me to follow. I was innovating as I went along – it was pure creation. Throughout this experience, I am not sure who learned more about leadership: me or my students.

The first week I was all excited to get started. The program began at 7:30 p.m. each night. I had the roster with me with all the names of the people who had registered. I was expecting about 50 people in the first class. At 7:30, I was at the front of the room sitting on my stool and there were only about 30 people in their chairs ready to go.

I was extremely disappointed as I felt they did not share the same enthusiasm I had, or they would all be waiting in their chairs raring, to get started. I just sat there and said nothing. Gradually people started to filter in. By 7:45 everyone was there except for one. I just sat there waiting. I could feel myself sweating. It was awkward for everyone and the silence was deafening. People were staring at me and I just sat there, unwavering. One person spoke out and asked when the program would get started. I replied, "It already has." My response did not go over well. People didn't understand and they were clearly getting agitated.

Finally, the last person showed up and took his seat.

I then asked, "How many of you have been on a plane before?"

Almost everyone raised their hand.

"How many have had the experience of showing up to the airport 15 minutes late for their flight, and then had the plane circle back to pick them up?"

To nobody's surprise, no one raised their hand.

We then discussed how the group felt that I had delayed the class for those who were late. Some were angry at me for wasting their time. Others were angry at the ones who showed up late. Of course, the tardy people gave the normal feeble excuses for why they were late. It was a very lively discussion and quite revealing for a lot of people.

To remind them of how things work when they show up late for an airplane, I told them that next week they should think of the classroom as a Boeing 737 airplane and class would start at the scheduled departure of 7:37 sharp. There would be no weather delays. At 7:37, I would close the door to the room and if they arrived and the doors were closed, we were already in the air so they could not come in. I changed the original time from 7:30 to 7:37 to remind them the classroom was now a Boeing 737 airplane.

The next week I went to the back of the room at 7:37 and closed the door. Everyone was in their seat ready to go except for two participants. I acknowledged those present for being on time and got started. No less than two minutes later, the doors opened, and a woman started to come in. I said, "I am sorry we are already at 10,000 feet, and you will have to catch the next flight." This lady lived in Kingston which was a two-hour drive away. She closed the door and left. The room went crazy.

"How could I send her home when she had driven two hours to get there?" they asked. I reminded them that I had driven four hours to get there, and she would get her own leadership lesson while driving back home. She was on time for every class after that and never held a grudge.

The man at the beginning of this story showed up for class at 8:00 p.m. that night. When he left after our encounter, we could hear a pin drop. People were stunned by what they just witnessed. We then started another conversation about being on time. I pointed out how much time had already been invested in the first two meetings just trying to get everyone together so we could get started. It was clear the class was starting to get impatient with my emphasis on timeliness. People were anxious to get started with the "true leadership program."

Then I explained that this exercise WAS part of the program. Being on time is the first step to honoring commitments and if people cannot count on you to keep your commitments you will not get far in life. Now I had their full attention, and they were intrigued by what else this program might reveal to them.

That was the last discussion we ever had about the importance of being on time and for the next six months we started at 7:37 sharp. No one ever even tried entering the closed door after the class started. I have no idea how many showed up late and then returned home. I suspect those that did learned another lesson.

At the end of that second class, I gave them an assignment: "Find someone in your life you do not know well and do something special for them every day for the next week." That was sure uncomfortable for a lot of them. I made sure the assignment was passed on to the two who were turned back.

Then the strangest thing happened. I started receiving daily gifts from someone with no name attached. The morning of the next class I received a call from someone's secretary, who asked to remain anonymous, inviting me to a complimentary dinner at 6:00 p.m. in the hotel where the class was being held. I had no idea who it was. I showed up for dinner a few minutes before 6:00 p.m. This was all very intriguing.

Much to my surprise, the belligerent man who had confronted me at the front of the room was sitting there waiting for me. He was the one who had been sending me gifts. He wanted to personally thank me for one of the biggest lessons he had ever learned. He acknowledged that he was always late for everything and no one ever called him out on it. He realized the cost it had on his life and his business. He was never late again. That was when I knew I was on the right track with this program.

Years later, when I was teaching my two-day marketing class, I would always start my class at 7:37 a.m. I never said why but was completely amazed at how making it start at that specific and somewhat unusual time dramatically changed the result. If I had advertised that the class would start at 7:30 or 8:00, people would assume we would start at "about" that time. By saying we would start at precisely 7:37, it gave real specificity and virtually everyone was in their chairs and ready to go. What a difference that made.

The UP Program turned out to be wildly successful. As everything was experiential, we all participated in different aspects of leadership during the program. There were no textbooks or reference materials to read. Every week I gave them an assignment to work on that would stretch them as individuals. These exercises developed their leadership abilities as individuals.

In the middle of the program, I gave the group a leadership challenge. First, I asked them to organize themselves in groups of 10. Then, they were to appoint a leader for their group. Just completing those two tasks was very revealing. They saw how they individually interacted in a group. Was their tendency to be a leader or a follower? How did they feel if they were not automatically selected to a group? Did they sit back and wait to be picked, or did they show up powerfully and ask to be selected?

I gave no instructions on how to select a leader. Some groups did it the "democratic way" by allowing each person to give their pitch on why they should be the leader and then they voted. Some groups just naturally looked to the person they thought would be the best leader and appointed them. One group had a leader who just declared he would be the best person for the job and if no one objected they would be the leader.

Once they had their group and their leader, I gave them an assignment.

1. Create a project that would be completed in three months.

2. This project must include every person on the team.

3. This project must provide a significant and ongoing benefit to the community; and

4. There is no budget for the project and if they need any funds to make it work, they will have to generate them on their own.

I was crystal clear that they needed to manage their time commitments and really stretch themselves.

Then I gave them two weeks to create their project and come back and present their idea to the group at large. (I had the two classes I was teaching together for this meeting). Then, the entire group had to vote on which project they felt had the most merit. Once that single project was selected, then every other team had to give up their project and back the winning project 100% and see it through to completion.

The group passed with flying colors and selected a project that still has a lasting impact today. The project leader of that group was a fiery red-headed woman named Chantal. She was French Canadian and an airline attendant. I realize now that because she worked for the airlines, she already knew the value of being on time. Chantal was one of the most passionate people I have ever met. She came up with the idea of planting 10,000 trees, and amazingly they pulled it off. She approached the Ontario Forestry Department with the idea and told them they had 100 volunteers to complete the task. They were given 10,000 seedlings and an area of forest that had been clear-cut.

How she negotiated all this with the Forestry Department, given her limited background, still astounds me. She went to the first meeting along with another team member who was an attorney. I suspect their enthusiasm and commitment to the details sold the forestry department on the idea. I doubt the forestry department had ever been approached by anyone with a project like this before.

None of us knew anything about planting trees and the forestry department showed us how to plant the seedlings to maximize their chance of success. The forestry department even provided some manpower of its own and committed to watering the trees after they were planted to ensure their continued growth and survival. I joined them for the planting and in two weekends we got it done. What a powerful experience that was.

What amazed me was that this one woman was able to mobilize 100 people to help her plant 10,000 trees. She had the forestry department completely on board. All of this was done in three months from conception to completion and not a single penny was spent by her or the group. I am extremely proud of the forest she and her group planted.

---♡---

What insights did I gain from this experience?

Honoring my time commitments is the same as honoring my word.

When I keep my agreements, I quickly gain the trust of others. The moment I start breaking my time commitments, is the moment I start losing credibility.

A project can be conceived and completed in an extremely short time frames when there is passion, vision, and a commitment from the entire team to the undertaking.

Passion can be so infectious it inspires others to internalize a vision and commit to a project — even when it is not their idea.

One person can dramatically alter the course of many lives with a single idea.

I learned that I could influence other people for the better when I trust my intuition and not judge people negatively. I also learned to trust my intuition when creating something from nothing.

9

THE HARDEST THING I HAVE EVER DONE

A cold, dreary day in Montreal
(@ITSLIZOJO /Via Instagram in the Montreal Gazette)

"In the depth of winter, I finally learned that within me lay an invincible summer."

– Albert Camus,
Nobel Prize winner in Literature at the age of 44

I t was a cold, dreary day in Montreal in the fall of 1980.

The sky was gray, and all the leaves had fallen to the ground. I was coming off a traumatic break up of a four-year long relationship while living in Montreal. I had no job, no savings, no car and nowhere to live.

I was completely lost.

My only assets were my tenacity and my degree in Physical Education (BPE) from the University of New Brunswick (with a specialty in recreation and a minor in business). I was not licensed to be a schoolteacher, but rather I was trained to work more in a community or business environment.

While I was getting my degree, I heard amazing things about the Ottawa Athletic Club (OAC). At the time it was recognized as the top private athletic club in Canada. It had indoor and outdoor tennis, squash, racquetball, indoor and outdoor pools, a huge indoor track with an impressive fitness center in the middle, physiotherapy, massage, a nutrition center, yoga, and spa services. In short, it had everything.

Ottawa Athletic Club – Canada's Premier Fitness Club

Since it was too painful to stay in Montreal and I had nothing to lose, I decided to move to Ottawa to start a new life. I borrowed my parents' Volkswagen camper and figured I could stay in a parking lot until I found a place to live.

I drove the two hours from Montreal to Ottawa on a Friday morning, with no real idea how this was all going to work out. During the drive I came up with a strategy to get hired at the Ottawa Athletic Club. I decided to go in unannounced to meet with the General Manager. I didn't want to risk calling for an appointment or mailing a resume in case I was rejected. I needed a job and I needed one today!

The moment I walked in the front door I was in awe. This was everything I imagined and more. I was greeted by a very fit young woman at the reception. I introduced myself and let her know I was there to speak to the General Manager (not even knowing his or her name). She asked if I had an appointment. I replied that I did not, but only needed five minutes, and I had a gift to give them.

She ushered me into the General Manager's office. He was a nice man in his early forties. I could tell right away he was aggravated by my showing up unannounced, and he was busy. I told him I was a recent graduate of UNB (which had a great reputation for their BPE program) and was looking for a job at the club. To which he replied, he had no openings, reached into his drawer, and pulled out a stack of resumes, and said each person was qualified. He said he could pick from any of them, so why should he offer me a job?

I told him my gift to him was one week of my services at absolutely no charge. If he liked my performance, I asked that he consider hiring me when the first opening came up. If he did not like what he saw, then he owed me nothing. Nobody had ever made that kind of irresistible offer to him before; he agreed on the spot.

As we were sitting in his office, his weekend manager called in sick and said she could not come in that night or the rest of the weekend. Synchronicity strikes again. He told me that if I could report back that afternoon, he would show me the ropes and I could start that night. I had to pinch myself to make sure I was not dreaming.

I worked all weekend, quickly picked up the job and got along well with everyone. On Monday morning, the same person who had called in sick called the manager back to announce that she was pregnant and needed to take a year off. After only two days of "free" labor I was given her job. It was only 12 hours a week, but I had my foot in the door and it was not long before I was promoted to a full-time position. Within eight months I was the Assistant Manager of the Fitness Department. I have no doubt that it was my willingness to do "whatever it takes" that caught the attention of the General Manager.

I found a place to live nearby where I could walk to work, and I returned my parents' camper. I would be renting a room in a family's house. The house was nothing special and a bit run down. My room was in the basement and it was dark, musty, and damp. The bed was like a waterbed – only it was not. It sagged so much in the middle I felt when I was sleeping in it, I was a hot dog in a bun. There was only one tiny window with no view. The room was adjacent to the TV room they had set up downstairs, as well as the laundry and furnace room. The walls were made of thin 4' x 8' wood panels attached to 2" x 4" studs. They were not insulated, so there was absolutely no privacy. It had a single, bare light bulb on the ceiling. But I had a place to stay that was close to work and it was cheap. Humble beginnings.

Meals were included with the rent, but they were so bad I only ate two meals there. The first meal was a fried steak that had been frozen and was smothered with greasy onions and green beans from a can.

The following week, all staff at the club had to take a course in CPR and that is when I met Debbie Prince. We fell in love immediately. It was not long after that I moved out of the dreary place I rented and moved into her apartment. We had a lot in common, as we were both into fitness and she also graduated from UNB a couple of years before me. In her teens, and all through university, she was one of Canada's top swimmers and eventually became my swim coach as I prepared to compete in the IRONMAN Triathlon World Championships. We just clicked and she was incredibly supportive of my fitness goals. She had retired from her swimming career after university, so she focused her attention on supporting me.

I have many fond memories of working at the Ottawa Athletic Club. It was the dream job for me and was a great fit for the training I had received with my degree.

At the time I was seriously into running and had already competed in a few marathons. I was inspired to start a running club that would be a division of the OAC. I thought it would be fun to have some running partners. It was an enjoyable recreational group and we named ourselves the OAC "Panters" (no, that is not a typo). Our mascot and logo were a caricature of the Pink Panther. Although we were committed to our training, we did not take ourselves too seriously and had lots of fun together. We had racing outfits and everything.

Later that year I led a group of them to Athens, Greece, to run the original marathon course which traced the steps of Pheidippides. Legend has it that in 490 B.C., Pheidippides ran from the plains of Marathon to the city of Athens to declare victory against the Persian army. He collapsed dead upon making the announcement. The race started in Marathon on the coast, and we ran uphill to Athens, passing by his tomb. We ran essentially the same route he did and finished in the original Olympic Stadium.

I will never forget rounding the corner and arriving at the entrance to the stadium to see my parents waving and holding a large Canadian flag.

**Greeted by my parents at the entrance to the original
Olympic Stadium in Athens, Greece**

The Olympic Stadium is carved out of white marble and has the long narrow track inside where gladiators would race their chariots. I got to run on that very track and did my best to absorb all the history in which I was immersed.

I looked up to see our running club banner hanging in the historic stadium. It was impossible to keep tears from flowing down my face. That was an incredibly emotional experience and I still get goosebumps reliving that memory. I have always wanted to compete in the Olympics, and never have, but at least I can say I competed in the original Olympic Stadium.

**Our running club banner hanging proudly in the
Olympic Stadium – in Athens, Greece**

Two years after we met, Debbie and I got married. We went to Hawaii for our honeymoon while I competed in the IRONMAN Triathlon. Not many wives would be willing to put up with all my training, much less have the event take place during our honeymoon. She did so willingly.

The only downside of working at the Ottawa Athletic Club was that the pay was not much more than minimum wage. About a year after I was hired, I got a job offer at almost double the pay. I was one of six fitness instructors who were hired to run a two-year-long study to determine how employee fitness affected productivity in a blue-collar setting.

The study was a joint project between Fitness Canada and The Canadian Public Health Association. That meant moving to Winnipeg, Manitoba, and I snatched it up. It was a great opportunity for me. I was posted at the Canada Safeway food distribution plant, which had 400 employees. The average employee profile was male, aged 40, smoked 40 cigarettes a day, was 40 pounds overweight, bet at least $40 on every Winnipeg Jets hockey game, and who knows how many beers he drank a week. I am proud to say that against all odds, my partner and I made a huge impact on that company, significantly improved their health and productivity, and reduced their absenteeism. Debbie moved with me and was able to secure a job assisting with the production of the Manitoba Marathon.

Over the course of the next ten years, I was changing jobs, changing cities, and taking risks – all with the intention of providing a better life for us and our two boys. We lived in six different cities and eight different homes. Some jobs worked out brilliantly and others were huge failures.

We went from our modest beginnings of sharing a small apartment to eventually buying a 4,600-square-foot mansion with all the trimmings on two acres, outside of Toronto. We had a new Jaguar XJ6, (my dream car), a new Mazda MPV, a $10,000 wardrobe, and a steady flow in income from a network marketing business I was involved with from the ground floor.

Within months of moving into our mansion, there was a change of ownership in the business. Unfortunately, the new owners were not able to effectively keep up product supply with a rapidly growing sales force. Within months it came tumbling down and our bonus checks went from $20,000 a month to a mere $2,000.

Debbie and I could no longer pay our bills. We lost everything. I filed for bankruptcy.

That was an extremely humbling experience, one that I wish on no one. I take full responsibility for that time, as I was the one handling the money and bringing in the income. Reflecting on that period in my life, I was more concerned about "looking good" than building a solid financial foundation. I was spending money faster than it was coming in.

With my tail between my legs, we moved again, this time to the United States to begin a new life. I started a seminar business in Vancouver, Washington, right across the river from Portland, Oregon. It was modestly successful, and we were renting a nice three-bedroom apartment. Our two sons, Graham and Tyler, were now nine and six years old.

If anyone had asked me how my relationship with my wife was at the time, I would respond by saying it was great. I felt that way because we would never fight. For many years it was a stable relationship. However, over time I discovered we had one fundamental difference. I was a risk-taker, and she was not. Neither is right or wrong, we just had a different make-up. I put her through a lot of turmoil, which when I look back on it, was not considerate of her desire to play safe.

I remember one day in 1986, I went to a seminar presentation on the advantages of being a vegetarian. I came home that night and declared I would not be eating meat anymore. I have not had a bite of meat since. I look back on that day now and realize I could have handled that situation a lot better. I did not take the time to find out how she felt about it and if she wanted to try that new lifestyle. Since she did most of the cooking that meant an additional burden on her to prepare two meals every time.

This is just one example of how we were slowly growing in different directions; the passion in our marriage was slowly dying. It was not that any one thing happened that I could say was a turning point. Rather our relationship changed with a series of small events over time.

There is a famous story of how a frog can be boiled without knowing it. If a frog is thrown into boiling water, it will instantly jump out. But, if a frog is placed in cold water, and the water is slowly brought to a boil, the frog will not jump out and eventually it will boil to death. That frog story depicts how our relationship was going. It happened so gradually that I did not even realize I was not happy in it anymore and was slowly drifting apart from my wife.

A year after moving to the United States, I was invited to assist at the Street Smart Business Camp. It was held in San Diego over

Thanksgiving weekend and there were more than 300 Canadians coming to the event. It was a five-day event that went from 6:00 a.m. to almost midnight every day. The motto of the camp was, "We can sleep next week!" I was working mostly in a support role. One of the volunteers was a beautiful lady named Janice Rule. I was instantly attracted to her, but of course since I was married, I knew that I could not pursue any kind of relationship. During the five days we were working side by side, and I just felt good to be with her.

On the last day, the camp culminated with a fire walk, which was to be a surprise to the participants. I had walked on fire several times before and was put in charge of preparing the coals. Two other guys helped me, and we had two cords of oak in a big pile that we set on fire in the parking lot, out of view of the participants. The fire was so hot that even with long handled shovels and bandanas over our face we could barely get close enough to the fire to move it around. Eventually, it burned down to a manageable level. We raked out the coals into three lines each about 20 feet long.

Once it was dark, the participants were told what was happening and were briefed on how this was going to work. They formed three lines of 100 people and one-by-one they walked across the coals. My job was to be at the front of one of the lines and put each participant through a series of breathing exercises and Neuro Linguistic Programming to get their mind right before they stepped out on to the hot coals. When I felt they were ready, I would send them off. If they were not, I would direct them to go to the back of the line and give it another try later. It was a tremendous responsibility. If I sent someone across the coals when they were not ready, they would surely burn their feet.

Since I had built the fire, there was no doubt in my mind that the coals were red hot. After we had sent all the participants through the fire-walk, the leader of the camp said it was now time for the staff to go, and he asked for some fresh coals. After sending all those people in front of me, I was both physically and emotionally spent. Combined with having only five hours sleep for the last five nights, I should have known better than to go. Plus, no one was checking me to be sure I was ready before I started my fire walk. I had nothing to prove since I had walked on fire before, but I went anyway. Big mistake. I can now attest to the fact that walking on fire can burn your feet. I burned them badly and could barely walk on them for a week.

I did not realize how bad it was until we were back in the seminar room and I started to get faint. Janice looked at me and intuitively knew something was wrong. She, and her friend Rich, took me to my room, bathed my feet, got a fresh Aloe Vera plant from outside, and treated my feet. Rich was an energy healer and he worked magic on my feet and released a lot of the heat within. While he was doing that, Janice made me something to eat to get my energy back up.

I felt totally taken care of. It was then that I started to fall in love with Janice. The next morning, I was back on a plane to Portland and when I arrived home, I realized that I truly felt like the frog in the water slowly boiling to death. I had to find a way to jump out before it was too late.

I could not get my mind off Janice and there was nothing I could do about it. I felt trapped in a marriage that was not bad – it was just that the life in our relationship was gone. I had two great kids and had made a commitment to be married to Debbie for the rest of my life. I had always lived by the philosophy that once I gave my word, I had to honor it. Being out of integrity was not an option. And yet, here I was, profoundly aware of how miserable I was. The internal turmoil was unbearable, and I had nobody I could even talk to about it.

A month later, the person who organized the Street Smart Business Camp, Harv Eker, called me and invited me to move to San Diego to help him launch the Street Smart Business School. It was a great opportunity but meant another move and transplanting my wife and kids yet again. I negotiated with him that I would do it on a trial basis for six months as long as I could go back to Vancouver every month for an extended weekend and teach my monthly seminar. At the end of six months, if everything worked out, I would move my family to San Diego. I was fortunate to have a great team of volunteers (including Debbie) that helped in the production of the seminars in Portland so I could come and go easily.

In January of 1996, I flew to San Diego on my own. I brought my bicycle, so I had some means of transportation. I rented a one-room studio in Cardiff by the Sea with a full-on view of the ocean. I could watch the whales go by while I was working from home. It was a magical experience and totally different from growing up in Canada.

Janice had been working at another company in Michigan which suddenly stopped doing business and she made her way back to San Diego. Harv hired her to help sell the seminars. This meant that we were working together side-by-side again, something that was not planned by either of us. I knew there must have been a grand plan to bring us back together. We went out for dinner one night and from that moment on I knew we were meant for each other.

Now my dilemma got bigger. I had found happiness again – but I was married to someone else. At the end of the first month, I returned to Vancouver to teach a seminar and that was when it really hit me. What I thought was a great relationship was not working for me anymore. I do not blame Debbie; it is just that I kept changing and we were going in different directions. I went back to Vancouver a few more times and each time the situation got worse. What I should have done was to man up, come clean, and tell her the truth about what was going on. I could not do it. I did not want to hurt her, or the kids. I knew the consequences for them and for me would be horrible. Plus, I had made a commitment to her and did not want to break it. I was torn up inside.

We were coming up to the end of the six-month trial period and the business was going great. The kids were finishing school and so it was time to make plans to have them move down to San Diego. I needed to find a house to rent. My situation was insane. I had no car in San Diego, so Janice was driving me around in her car helping me find a place to rent so I could bring my family down there to live. I found a nice house and signed a one-year lease to start on July 1. I was going to go back to Vancouver to finish packing up our apartment, go camping for a week with Debbie and the kids, and then drive down to San Diego to start another chapter.

I do not know what I was thinking. I was carting them off to yet another place to fit my needs, not theirs. I had strong feelings for

Janice but had not said anything to Debbie. I think she suspected something was going on, but it was never addressed. I know I feared that truth and she probably was fearing it, too.

The plans were all set for the move and as I got on the plane one last time to go to Vancouver, I knew I had to address the truth – that was I was in love with Janice. I spent the whole plane ride trying to figure out what to say. That was the plane ride from hell. I did not want to hurt her, but I also knew I could no longer stay married to her. There is no easy way to speak that truth and no creative way of saying it that was going to soften the blow.

That night I waited until the kids were asleep and broke the news to her. No surprise – it did not go well. Here we were, the apartment was all packed up, we had a home to move to in San Diego, and we were committed to that plan. The next morning, she asked if we could work on the marriage and see if we could make it work. I agreed out of respect for her and my kids. We went on our camping trip and it was torture. I did not want to be there, but the kids knew nothing about what was going on, so I had to keep up appearances. Eventually, we loaded up the U-Haul with everything we owned. I drove it with one son in the front seat with me and Debbie followed in the car with the other one. That was an excruciatingly long three-day drive.

On the last night before we arrived in San Diego, we found a cheap motel in Bakersfield. Debbie put the kids to bed, and we had a frank talk. She gave me an ultimatum. She said she did not feel I was 100% committed to making the marriage work. (She was right). She then said that she wanted a decision that night. Either I was going to commit 100% to making the marriage work, which included never seeing Janice again, or we were done. Logistically that was a challenge, since Janice and I worked together, but I knew what she meant.

I left the hotel room about 11:00 p.m. and walked the streets of Bakersfield trying to decide the direction of my life. Believe me, that is no place to make a life-altering decision at that time of night. I was in a rough part of the neighborhood and feared for my life as I was not the only person walking the streets and I sure looked like I did not fit there. There was no question about what I wanted to do.

I wanted to be with Janice. But making that decision dramatically impacted the lives of my wife and kids. I had to decide quickly. The choice was between living with happiness or keeping my agreements.

If I were a person who did not value integrity as much as I do, the decision would have been a lot easier. I wondered what kind of example I would be setting for my kids. I also had to consider how this would affect Debbie, given the promises I had made to her. The internal pressure was immense. I could not slow down my heart, and my head was pounding. I was having a hard time breathing. After walking the streets for more than an hour I found a payphone and called Janice. Fortunately, she answered. I have no idea what I said, but just hearing her voice was enough. I made up my mind and went back to the hotel and told Debbie I could not honor her request. We were done.

The next day was awkward, to say the least. The kids still had no idea of what was going on. Janice had previously arranged for a few people from work to meet at our home to help us unpack. I called her and said that probably was not a good idea. We arrived at the house for which I had just signed a one-year lease and unpacked the truck into the garage. All of Debbie's things and the kids' things were put on the left side and my clothes, a dresser, my computer, one lamp that was a wedding present from my cousin, and my sound system for seminars went on the right.

Debbie did not have a work visa for the United States and had no connection to San Diego, so she decided to move back to Canada and took the kids with her. She arranged for a moving truck, which arrived two days later. Everything was happening so fast.

She told me that since I had created this mess it was my job to tell the kids.

That was the hardest thing I have ever had to do.

With my two sons, Graham and Tyler - 1993

I took them to a park and did my best to break the news to them. Graham and Tyler were 10 and 7 at that time. They took it better than I thought they would, but doing it ripped a hole in my heart. I doubt they fully grasped what was happening at the time and how it would impact our lives. They wanted to know why they had to move back to Canada and why I was staying in San Diego. I kept telling them I loved them no matter what. I really did not know what else to say.

Just like that, the next day they were gone. I had to call the landlord and let her know I would not need the house. She was very understanding of the situation and let me out of the one-year lease by just paying one month's rent.

A couple of weeks later I flew to Ottawa and helped secure a townhome for Debbie and the boys. I painted the inside, so it was clean for them. That week is a complete blur. I cannot even remember where I stayed. I certainly was not welcome with my family. By the time I flew back to San Diego, I felt like the life had been sucked out of me.

Now the rebuilding process of my life began – yet again – for the third time.

I had no place to live, and almost no money. Being homeless is no fun. I stayed with some good friends for a few days and then Janice invited me to move in with her. She had just secured a 385-square-foot guest house that was in the back of someone's property. She was so excited to have a place of her own that was her "Zen" place. This would be a place where she could have quiet time and meditate. Then I showed up and everything changed.

We had a queen bed, a small table and 4 chairs, and my dresser, all crammed into the living space. It had a pot-belly stove for heat which was so close to the bed we had to be careful the bed did not catch on fire.

The kitchen area had a half-sized refrigerator, a microwave, a hot plate, and a sink. There was one cupboard for dishes which doubled as the pantry, and one drawer for cutlery. If you looked up the definition of a "Chef's Kitchen" in the dictionary you would not find a picture of this kitchen in there.

The bathroom was tucked into a corner and had saloon doors leading into it. Not ideal for privacy. The corner shower was so small that I had to turn sideways to get into it.

We shared a small yard with the tenant in the main house, so we had a little breathing room when it got too close inside.

The accommodations did not matter. The main thing was that I was living with Janice. Although not seeing my kids resulted in a heavy heart, I could start to feel happy and took on the challenge of rebuilding again.

I had made a commitment to Debbie to send her $2,000 a month to help support the kids. Debbie was understandably hurt and angry with me when I told her about my relationship with Janice. She shared what I had done with many of my key clients in Vancouver. As a result, my seminar support team was not willing to assist with the production of my seminars anymore, so that source of income came to a screeching halt.

A few weeks later, a marketing consulting contract I had with an eyewear company was unexpectedly cancelled, thereby ending another source of income.

Then a couple of weeks after that, Harv called us into his office and told us he was shutting down the school, which ended our contract.

In the space of about three weeks all three sources of my income, suddenly and without warning, dried up. I wanted to send money to my kids, but now I had no income and no immediate possibility to get any. It felt like someone had pulled the rug out from under me and life was unravelling fast. Janice had lost her job too, so we had to figure this out together.

Janice had been attending numerous networking meetings, which were primarily geared for women. She soon recognized that many of these women owned small businesses or were in the healing profession and had no clue how to market their business or services effectively. She immediately saw that as our ticket, and we created a seminar called *7 Steps to Marketing Mastery – for women only.* I give Janice full credit for coming up with that idea. It was brilliant.

Our tiny living space soon became our office, too, and we started selling the course. With our backs up against the wall, it is amazing how resourceful we became. We made up a flyer and took it to Kinkos to have 100 copies run off on colored paper. We did not even have the money for stamps, so Janice would give the flyers out at the networking meetings. Once we had our first enrollment, we had more flyers printed and kept marketing. Janice was primarily responsible for selling out the course and we co-led the course. It was wildly successful, and we are still in touch with some of the participants in our first course.

That course was the beginning of a seminar business that did well for 10 years.

The first few years after I split up with Debbie were extremely painful. I was only able to speak to my kids twice a week. Each time I called, I had to listen to Debbie verbally abusing me for ten minutes before I was able to speak to the kids. As much as I looked forward to speaking with my kids, I dreaded making those calls.

I remember days and nights lying in bed where my heart hurt so bad, I could barely breathe. A turning point in my healing process was listening to an audio recording by the singer Kenny Loggins – only he was not singing. He was sharing how his life was turned upside down and how he rebuilt it with people around him who truly supported him. His old friends and managers were extremely upset with him because of the choices he made and told him, "He had the nerve to seek happiness." I replayed that tape many times and am so glad I chose happiness.

Once we had our divorce settled, I had visitation rights for the kids for the summers and alternating Christmas and Spring Breaks. They would spend each summer with us, which I loved. Janice did not have children of her own and enjoyed having the kids with us.

My younger son Tyler gravitated more to me and shared the same entrepreneurial traits I have. He is now part of our business, owns two homes around the corner from us, and is doing extraordinarily well.

My older son Graham chose to follow more in his mother's footsteps and has remained in Ottawa. As much as I would like to have a relationship with him, I need to honor and respect his decisions. He has chosen not to communicate with me in any way for almost five years now. Father's Day, birthdays and Christmas are still painful, and I hope that one day we will be able to heal our differences together. In the meantime, I just keep sending him love and positive energy.

Janice and I recently celebrated our 22nd wedding anniversary. We got to celebrate it with some dear friends at our new mountain retreat. I am so proud of how far we have come from those humble beginnings of living together in 385-square-feet. Together we make an unstoppable team.

---♡---

What insights did I gain from this experience?

It is always better to speak the truth, even when I am fearful of the consequences.

Delaying difficult conversations only worsens a painful situation. It is better to pull off the Band-Aid in one quick pull, rather than trying to pull it off slowly.

Take responsibility when things go wrong and allow for corrections to be made.

It is only when I take full responsibility for my actions that I can make any changes. Blaming others for my circumstances does no good. I alone created them, and it is up to me to create the circumstances I desire.

The size of my house, or the car I drive, does not equate to my happiness.

Happiness is a choice. I can choose to be happy regardless of my situation. The people I choose to share my life with greatly enhance my happiness.

Having a life partner who shares my hopes and aspirations is priceless.

Janice is a huge reason for my success in life. Being able to share my life with her makes it all worthwhile.

10
THE CHRISTMAS TREE STORY

Our Christmas Tree all decorated - Palomar Mountain, CA 2020

"Be a light in the darkness."

– Ancient Wisdom

A Christmas tree has a different symbolic meaning for many people.

Growing up in Canada it was always exciting for me to peek into the living room on Christmas morning to see what presents we might find under the tree. We always had a real tree with colored lights and lots of ornaments. My brother and sister and I we were always up early that morning and eager to rip open the wrapping paper. My parents did an incredible job to make as big a display of gifts as they could afford.

One thing we could always count on was a new hockey stick and skates. The skates were usually bought at a secondhand sports store and exchanged for last year's skates, as we were growing so quickly. Another staple we could count on was new flannel pajamas, socks, and underwear, and if we were lucky, a toy or two.

The thrill of receiving gifts and opening up new stuff never got old. I remember going to a small gift shop in the village to buy something for my parents each year and I looked forward to watching their reactions as they opened their present. It was a big deal for me to be able to buy something for them. I saved my allowance money, along with money earned from doing odd jobs.

Christmas was also a time where family gathered together to celebrate. We usually went to a Church Choir service late on Christmas Eve and return to our home afterward, where we were allowed to open just one gift. Even though we wanted to, we could not light a fire in the fireplace or Santa Claus would get burned coming down the chimney. We would leave out cookies and milk for Santa and a carrot for Rudolph, the red-nosed reindeer. I am sure my Dad thoroughly enjoyed the cookies.

There never seemed to be many presents under the tree on Christmas Eve, yet by some miracle, Santa would arrive after we went to bed, and we would wake up and there would be presents everywhere. Those were some happy times and the Christmas tree for me was symbolic of those good times.

We always had a real tree, and I loved the smell of it. The tradition of bringing in a fresh Christmas pine continued until we traveled to Nigeria when I was eleven. Living near the Sahara Desert meant there was no traditional Christmas tree within thousands of miles. We innovated and decorated a small palm tree with a string of tiny white lights. Instead of hockey sticks and skates that year, we got tennis rackets, balls, and tennis shoes.

As I grew up and had sons of my own, I kept the tradition going. I remember one year driving out into the country with a hand saw where we walked through deep snow to find the perfect tree. After careful selection we cut it down. dragged it back to the car and took it home. Some years were good financially and others were lean, but we always seemed to manage to have money to buy presents and wrap them, so the boys were never disappointed.

Somewhere along the way I seemed to equate the number of gifts under the tree as to how successful a year we had financially. In my late twenties I was so happy and proud to be able to gift my Dad a brand new snow blower. This was something he would never buy for himself. It was also a far cry from the little trinkets I could afford to buy my parents when I was a kid.

The year I separated from my wife Debbie was a completely different experience of Christmas. She had moved back to Canada with the kids. I was living with Janice in San Diego and there was no snow in sight. Worst of all, we were flat-out broke, and I was separated from my children. There was no money for Christmas presents, much less a tree. My kids were 3,000 miles away and none of my family were talking with me due to their judgments about my leaving my wife and kids. This was not the Christmas I was used to. I felt like a total failure and totally alone. My saving grace was being with Janice. She was giving me huge amounts of joy, even during this time of pain and chaos in my life.

On Christmas Eve, Janice and I decided to go for a long walk. We happened to walk past an outdoor Christmas-tree lot. We lingered outside the fence and longed for a tree of our own to start our new traditions together. But we just did not have any money.

A nice man, who I suspect was the owner of the lot, came over and asked if he could help us. We thanked him but said we had no money to buy a tree. He looked at us compassionately and told us to go and pick out any tree we wanted – it was his gift to us. Tears welled up in my eyes. There was a Christmas spirit after all. He had no idea what a difference he just made in my life. I don't even know his name, yet he must have sensed that we needed a tree way more than any profit he would have made.

Since the place we were living in was so small we picked the smallest tree we could find and carried it home. It was truly a "Charlie Brown" tree, but it was just what we needed. Janice's mother had given us a box of Fannie Mae chocolates from Chicago (our only gift that year), so we wrapped it up and quickly walked back to the tree lot and gave it to the nice man. That was the first year in my life where there were no presents under the tree, and I will never forget it. It was a humbling experience.

I realized that everything I assumed about the relationship between how many gifts were under the tree and how successful a year I had was all made up. The truth was, that year I had no money, but lots of love in my heart from Janice. I realized I did not need a gift from anyone to feel love. At the same time, I never wanted to experience the feeling again of not being able to buy a tree.

Every year, as we put up our tree, I remember that one moment at the tree lot and acknowledge how far I have come. It truly was a defining time in my life. I also remember how a compassionate man gave us a tree when we needed it most. We were complete strangers to him. I realize he probably would never have been able to sell it past that night, but his simple gesture made a huge difference in my life and I will never forget it.

With new traditions in place for Christmas each year, we always do something for those less fortunate. Some years we have picked a family in need and been their "Secret Santa." Other years we have collected items for veterans and delivered them on Christmas.

A few years ago, we put an announcement in our local newsletter that we were collecting new shoes and socks for veterans. On Christmas Eve, my son Tyler, and his fiancée Mandie, arrived at our home with two dozen pairs of new running shoes they had purchased to donate. The next day we delivered them along with all the generous gifts from our community to a veteran's transition home. I was so pleased that Tyler and Mandie had embraced the spirit of "giving back" instead of just looking to see what presents would be waiting for them under the tree.

I believe that giving back is the true spirit of Christmas.

This year we celebrated Christmas at our beautiful new retreat on top of Palomar Mountain, just north east of San Diego. Right outside our living room window is a 20-foot tall pine tree – it is a perfect Christmas tree. No need to cut it down, we just enjoyed it from our window. It took a long pole and some creativity to string the lights and it took a while, but I savored every moment.

As I look at it, all lit up, I reflect on the significance of the Christmas tree and acknowledge how far we have come.

---♡---

What Insights did I gain from this experience?

A single act of compassion has the ability to affect a person's life forever.

The gift of that small Christmas tree, from a complete stranger, and the compassion that came with it, was a life-altering experience for me. Now I look to see how I can continue to pay it forward to others with simple acts of compassion.

Christmas is not just about how many presents are under the tree.

Christmas is about sharing love. For me, a Christmas tree is simply a symbol of that love.

11

PURSUING A DREAM –
THE PGA TOUR

At Fairbanks Ranch Country Club, 2000

*"The most rewarding things you do in life are often
the ones that look like they cannot be done."*

– Arnold Palmer, Legendary Golfer – "The King"

I was 44 years old and going through what I like to call "Mid-Life Clarity." I felt unsatisfied in what I was doing, even though I was good at it. I was bored. I felt it was time for a complete change of careers.

I had a successful seminar and coaching business. I was a business and success coach long before coaching was a thing. I had been doing this for more than 10 years and the struggle of continually filling seminars was taking a toll on me.

My coaching clients all had their unique challenges but to me there was nothing new, and they all started to look the same. Janice could tell I was stale, but I just kept pushing on, thinking I had few other options. I needed to pay the bills, and this seemed to be the best option. She kept asking me, "What do you really want to do with your life?" I had no answers.

Then I remembered a dream goal I had when I was 26 years old. I had wanted to play golf on the Professional Golfers Association Tour (the PGA TOUR).

I had learned to play golf when I was 12, living in Nigeria, of all places. I played for a couple of years on a course that barely resembled a golf course – it was complete with goat herders crossing the course at the most inopportune times.

Golf came naturally to me. When I started my life insurance career, I was invited to play in the annual London Life company golf tournament. I had to rent clubs and had not played in years but managed to score better than most of the guys who played regularly.

At the time, I was in demand as a speaker and was going all over Canada giving inspirational talks about my experience competing in the IRONMAN, and how I applied the athletic training principles into business. I had given dozens of talks and always loved sharing my message and inspiring others. I thought it would be amazing to be on the PGA TOUR and give a free talk in every city I played in. This would be my way of giving back.

Then my first child Graham came along in 1983, and I had the stress of selling life insurance. Insurance is probably the hardest thing on the planet to sell – I would put it right up there with charging Hawaiians for sunlight. Nobody wants to talk to you about dying!

I did very well at it, but with a new child at home and another on the way, time for me to golf was reduced to once or twice a year. My fleeting dream of playing on the tour was put in the "probably never going to do this" pile. I stuffed it away.

Until that fateful night when the memory was rekindled. I had a vivid dream and I saw myself walking down a fairway, alongside Tiger Woods and Phil Mickelson. The fairways were lined with thousands of fans and I was inside the ropes playing with two golf legends. The sky was blue, and the smell of the freshly cut grass filled my nostrils. I heard the sounds of the crowd as they hurried to get ahead of us in order to get a good view. The camera crew was close behind us, and I could hear them talking to the color commentators. Everything was crystal clear. What a rush!

The next morning, I shared with Janice my goal of playing on the PGA TOUR. Her first reaction was, "Where did that come from? You hardly even play golf." At the age of 44 and never having broken 80 in my life, this definitely did not seem to be a reasonable goal. Of course, that had never stopped me before.

Janice became an avid supporter of my goal, however, and backed me 100%. There is absolutely no way the rest of this story would have unfolded without her un-wavering support. I cannot express how fortunate I am to have a wife who supports my goals and dreams, even when they look like they cannot be done.

I decided to make my dream a reality. I was not going to let it go this time. I was not going to spend the rest of my life wondering if I was good enough to compete with the best golfers in the world.

My first step was to assess what I needed to achieve my goal. I boiled it down to three immediate things: I needed a place to play, I needed a coach, and I needed some golf clubs. Golf is not a cheap sport – all of this cost a great deal of money. Again, while I did not have the answers, I just pressed forward. As with any big endeavor, I soon found there were many other things I would need along the way, but I started with those three. I could only focus on what I could see in front of me, not what may be waiting for me over the horizon.

I started out by finding someone to license my seminars. That step created a residual income from my seminar business, and also relieved that work responsibility so I could just focus on golf.

A few years earlier, when Janice and I had decided to get married, we had a hard time securing a venue we liked. One of her good friends, Jo Merritt, was a member at the exclusive Fairbanks Ranch Country Club next to Rancho Santa Fe, California. Her husband, Tag Merritt, was the Director of Golf at the club. With their assistance, we were able to have a beautiful wedding ceremony overlooking the scenic course and a special reception in The Founders Room.

Tag mentioned there was a tradition at the club that if you got married there, you got to play a free round in the morning with him and two guests. Naturally, I jumped at the opportunity and had a great time. I still remember sinking a 60-foot putt on the last hole to win all the money. It must have been an omen. I had my best round ever shooting 81. Fairly good – but a far cry from PGA-caliber golf.

The morning I declared my goal to Janice she went for a walk with Jo and told her about what I wanted to do. Jo's exact words were, "He is crazy!!" She went on to stress, "Doug has no idea how impossible that is. He is in his forties and he doesn't even play. There is no way he can compete against guys in their 20's, who have been playing since they could walk." Of course, when Janice told me that, it fueled my desire even more.

That night, I called Tag and told him my goal. I also shared the three things I needed. He was gracious enough not to laugh out loud (which he should have, since he had seen me play). Nor did he try to steal my dreams by trying to talk me out of it. I will always be indebted to him for that and for constantly supporting me in pursuit of my goal. He said he would love to coach me but could not, since I was not a member at the club. However, he said he would do whatever he could to help.

True to his word, exactly one week later, he called me early in the morning and asked me, "Are you any good on the computer, are you good at organizing things and are you good working with all kinds of people?" I said yes to all three. He told me that in a few moments they would be firing the Golf Operations Manager and that I should apply for the job, as it would give me playing privileges at the club. He told me to call the General Manager without mentioning his name and tell him that I was applying for a job in the golf business, and that I was excellent at organizing events, was a whiz on the computer and loved working with people. I made the call and had my interview at 2 p.m. that same day.

Instead of meeting in his office, the General Manager gave me a tour of the club and we finished in The Founders Room where Janice and I had our wedding reception. He motioned for me to sit down and I went to the exact same seat where our head table was. It was kind of spooky, but I knew this was another good omen. I was hired immediately and started the next morning at 7:00. All of this transpired in one week after setting my goal.

I had full playing privileges at the club except for Tuesday and Thursday mornings, which were reserved for Ladies only. My job normally required about 30 hours of work a week, except for a few major tournaments a year where we worked long hours. They paid me $40,000 a year and I got free lunch every day in the members' restaurant.

The cost to join the club at the time was $85,000. Members also had monthly dues, including bar and restaurant minimums, totaling over $1,000. This was quite a package I just secured. I would have done the job for nothing, just for the privilege of being able to practice on a PGA TOUR- caliber course. I remember driving in to work the first morning, pinching myself wondering if this was all real. I was living my dream.

Now I had one of my three parts accomplished – I had a place to play. Now I just needed a good set of clubs and a coach. I was on my way and super excited.

About a week later, I was walking through the pro shop and the sales rep from TaylorMade was there making his best pitch to Tag to have him carry TaylorMade clubs and products in the shop. For some reason Tag did not like TaylorMade equipment. He was a big fan of Ping and Titleist and I could see the poor guy was getting nowhere fast. So, I casually walked behind them and said to Tag, "Are you getting me those clubs I need?" The rep's ears perked up and asked me, "Do you need some clubs?" I nodded and suggested he meet me in my office when he was done.

At that point, I had been at the club only a week and still had never broken 80 in my life. But, when the rep came to my office, I shared with him my goal of being on the PGA TOUR and that I needed a new set of clubs. I also suggested that if I were playing with TaylorMade, maybe it would start to sway the members and he could eventually have Fairbanks Ranch Country Club as one of his clients.

He seized the opportunity and set up a private fitting for me at the TaylorMade Kingdom in Carlsbad, California. The worldwide TaylorMade headquarters and manufacturing facility are right next door. The Kingdom is where all the sponsored PGA players come to try out new clubs and get fitted. At the time I had no idea what a big deal it was to get an invitation. Sometimes being naive can work to my benefit. A few days later I arrived and after going through a whole security check I was escorted to this fancy clubhouse and fitting center. Talk about exclusive!

When I walked in the lobby there were life-size photos of all the PGA TOUR players TaylorMade sponsored. Then I was ushered into the locker room and each player had his own name in brass on the locker. Right beside the one reserved for Ernie Els was a locker with my name on it for a day. They sure know how to treat clients like a king there.

My personalized locker for the day

Then we went into the fitting area and I was introduced to the club fitter who works with all the pros. He was a master at his craft and treated me like a pro. The facility was incredible. It was set up with a huge garage door that faced out onto a pristine driving range. The grass was emerald green and perfectly manicured. There was not a ball on it. Inside there was a hitting mat and 16 still cameras and several video cameras set up to record my swing. One of the cameras could take a photo of the ball compressed on the clubface as I hit it. That way we could see exactly where I was striking the ball on the clubface. Amazing.

They captured video from all angles that traced my clubhead during my swing and it was projected onto a large screen. The fitter could put my swing on a split screen and compare it side-by-side to any of the tour pros I wanted. I was like a kid in a candy store, while still trying to maintain some composure.

After a couple of hours of analysis and selecting different shafts and clubheads specifically fitted for me, he said my new clubs would be delivered directly to my office at the country club.

I did not want to push my luck, but I asked it if would be possible to get a bag as well since I would be promoting TaylorMade at the club. Without batting an eye, he said, "Sure – what style do you want?" I told him just a lightweight "carry bag" as I normally walk the course. At that time, I did not have the luxury of having a caddy to carry my clubs.

Three days later this huge box from Taylor Made arrived at the country club and I rushed to my office to open it. My new golf clubs were beautiful. I loved the copper-colored heads – they were so distinct.

Then I realized there was no bag with them. That took me aback – I did not know what to do. I checked the packing slip and there was no record of the bag. I thought maybe it was back-ordered and would arrive later. I mustered up my courage and called for the man that fitted me, but he was out of the office.

His assistant asked how she could help. I sheepishly inquired about the bag and she said, "Oh Mr. Davidson, please be patient, it takes six-to-eight weeks to have your name stitched on your bag." I replied, "I did not order a Tour Bag. I just need a carry bag."

The next day the carry bag was delivered. Then six weeks later, this huge box arrived for me and sure enough it was a Tour Bag with my name on it! I was stunned. I now felt like I belonged on the Tour. I was playing with the exact set of clubs that PGA Champion Ernie Els was playing with and I had my own bag with my name on it. I felt I would fit right in on the PGA TOUR. The best part was that all of this was a complete gift to me.

The next year when the new line of clubs came out, they fitted me again with their latest model, the "Tour 300." To top it all off, TaylorMade got their foot in the door at Fairbanks Ranch, and it was a win for everyone.

Two out of three things checked off by that point. Now I needed a coach, as I had never had a private lesson in my life. To my great fortune, Lynn Adams, a winning golfer on the LPGA TOUR, worked in the pro shop and gave lessons to the members. Lynn graciously agreed to teach me. I guess this was her way of giving back to someone who wanted to play at the same level she had achieved.

On the first day of lessons, we jumped into a golf cart and drove to the far end of the range. This area was reserved for private lessons and was available for me to use anytime I wanted. All the balls I could hit were neatly stacked into pyramids. She looked at my swing and we went to work. She changed my grip, my stance, my set-up, my back-swing, and my follow through – essentially everything I did as a golfer. I started out completely fresh. Lynn was a huge help and I learned so much from her.

Near the end of my first lesson an older gentleman drove up in a cart. He was very unassuming, and Lynn just said, "good morning" and carried on. He quietly went about his business. I watched him hit a few balls and his swing was silky smooth. He looked to be in his 70's but the ball just rocketed off his clubface and the sound was so crisp each time he hit it. I looked over at his bag and in big letters saw **Gene Littler** stitched on the side. Gene is in the PGA Hall of Fame, won the 1961 US Open and has 29 PGA Tour wins. Later in the clubhouse I saw a framed scorecard of his when he set a club record for the lowest score at Fairbanks Ranch – 64. No pressure at all, getting a lesson right beside a legend!

There were many days I would be practicing when Mr. Littler would come out and work on perfecting his craft. We soon became friends. He was a gentle soul and was always willing to answer my questions when asked. He made me feel like I was already on the Tour and one of the guys.

It wasn't long before had my first round in the 70's. Within six months I was shooting par on a regular basis. Then one day Janice's friend, Jo – the one who thought I was crazy – came into my office and said her playing partner had to cancel and invited me to play with her. I birdied the first hole and was on fire that day. I was sinking putts from everywhere. My drives were pure and right down the middle. I shot 69. The look on Jo's face was priceless. She never said a word, but it was an extremely gratifying moment for me. To shoot 69 on that course is Tour level!

Approaching the 18th Green at Fairbanks Ranch Country Club

My next challenge was to pass the PGA Players Ability Test (or PAT). This would allow me to start on the path of being a PGA member, enroll in the teaching program, and eventually get a PGA card. PGA members typically can play at any course they want for free. I thought that would be a nice perk, so I signed up for the next test.

The PAT was held at a local course and one of my buddies agreed to caddy for me. The way the test worked was that I had to play 36 holes in one day and shoot below a certain number (depending on the difficulty of the course). That day, the number was six over par for the 36 holes. I figured I could do that! Turns out it was way harder than it looked. There was the pressure of the day and each time I had a bad hole, the pressure got worse. I failed miserably. The fact that only 10% of the entrants passed the test was no consolation to me.

I went back to work on my game and tried again at a private club in Brentwood (just outside of Los Angeles) a few months later. I had my first hole-in-one that day and it was perfect because the clubhouse was closed on Monday – so I didn't have to buy any drinks. Even with my hole-in-one, I still missed qualifying by four shots.

A couple of months later, I tried once again at a course in Palm Springs. Janice came with me to be my caddy. She did not know much about the technical parts of golf but was superb at grounding me and keeping me focused. As we pulled into the parking lot, we noticed three young guys peeling into the parking lot. They got out of their car and were eating left-over pizza and drinking Big Gulps in preparation for the tournament. Much to my chagrin, that is who I was paired with.

It turned out they were terrible golfers. Soon they were cursing and throwing their clubs. This sure was a major distraction for me and I used up all my "above par" strokes in the first 18 holes. I then had to shoot even par on the next 18 holes to qualify. I decided to just take one hole at a time and play conservative golf. Just aim for the middle of the fairway, the center of the green, make two putts and get off the green. It worked like a charm. I racked off 14 consecutive pars. All the while, Janice and I were doing our best to stay in our own bubble and ignore the guys we were paired with.

On the 15th hole I hit the green and had a 20-foot putt which I left about 18 inches short. I walked up to casually tap it in – And I missed it. I could not believe I blew it – the challenge just got immense. I had three holes to go and had to make two pars and a birdie to qualify. The next hole was a par three and I hit my tee shot to within 6 feet. I was excited, thinking *Here's my birdie*. I misread the line and it lipped out. Par.

The next hole was a par five. When I played it in the morning, I was not able to reach the green in two. As I walked up to the tee box, out of nowhere the wind came up from behind me. Mother

Nature was on my side. I hit a towering drive right down the middle of the fairway and then hit a perfect 3-wood right at the green. Since I had a tail wind behind me, the ball rolled right through the green and settled in a bunker on the other side. Fortunately, I had a good lie, and I blasted the ball out of the sand to within three-feet of the hole. I then settled in, calmed my nerves, and made my birdie putt. I was back on track. After playing 35 holes and enduring the terrible company we had that day, and despite two previously unsuccessful attempts, it all came down to one hole. If I made a par, I qualified. If I did not, it was back to trying again for the fourth time. No pressure!

The last hole was a relatively easy, uphill par 4. I hit my drive right down the middle and had an easy wedge shot from about 80 yards. Then I did the unthinkable. I chunked my shot and left it 20 yards short of the green. Now I only had two shots left to get on the green and sink my putt. I did my best to calm myself. I hit a fairly good chip. Right online, but it rolled a long eight feet past the hole. I let the other three guys finish up, as they were out of it anyway. I just focused. Janice was off to the side of the green calling in all the golf gods and angels.

I circled the hole twice, making sure I had a good read. It looked like a straight putt. I got over the ball and lined myself up. Then my throat went completely dry. I backed off and centered myself again. Then as I lined up again, my eyes started to water. What was happening? I stepped back wiped my eyes, cleared my throat, and centered myself. I was experiencing a real pressure putt for the first time in my life. Now I could understand how the pros can miss short, seemingly routine putts, when under extreme pressure. I lined up again and visualized the ball dropping in the cup. I made my stroke and the ball rolled 8-feet and dropped right in the heart of the cup.

I was elated and jumping for joy. I did it! I was legit! I had passed the Players Ability Test.

What a confidence booster making that putt was, and many times later when facing pressure putts, I would relive that moment. That visualization and that memory sure helped.

That experience told me it was time to play in some competitions. Unfortunately, most of the entry fees were steep and I did not have the extra money to register. Then one day I was playing with one of the club's older members. He was a genuinely nice Greek man, but not many members wanted to play with him. It would often take him 2 or sometimes 3 shots just to get to where my drive would land. Most people did not have the patience to play with him, and he just did not fit in with the crowd.

As time went on, he asked me to play with him several times. The two of us got to talking on a round one day and I was sharing my goal and how I wished I could play on the Mini Tours to hone my game. He very generously agreed to give me $500 every month to help. Each month I would meet him at the post office, and he would give me an envelope with five crisp $100 bills in it. He never asked for anything in return and never wanted anyone at the club to know he was helping me, which is why we always met off-site. He was another angel who entered my life.

During my year as a professional golfer, I played in as many local tournaments as I could, and each one was a learning experience. Soon after the Pepsi Tour was formed, I decided to join it. It was a developmental tour played all over Southern California that provided a competitive environment for aspiring golfers. I so loved the competitive side of the game and the fact that it was completely me against the course. I was fortunate to win one tournament on the Pepsi Tour.

However, I soon learned that playing golf recreationally with your buddies is one thing and playing golf for money is something entirely different. The pressure is intense. Although the players I was competing against were cordial enough, it was definitely a competition, and everyone was out to win.

Completely different from the many sports teams I had played, golf is a solitary sport, and no fellow golfers were going to assist or cheer me on. I was on my own. When things didn't go my way on the golf course, which was often the case, it was completely up to me and my own mental fortitude to fight through it. I learned to focus only on the next shot.

I was fortunate that while working at the club, I was able to meet Phil Mickelson and walk a round of golf with him as he practiced.

I learned so much from him that day. On one hole, he showed me three different types of approach shots from about 30 yards from the pin. Remarkably all three ended up within five feet of the hole. Phil is internationally regarded for his short game – he is truly a wizard. It is one thing to watch him on television, it is another to be standing beside him while he makes yet another miracle shot, while making it look routine. I studied how he practiced and what his strategy was on each hole. Being in the presence of a true master is always inspiring.

With Phil Mickelson, 2001

I can only imagine what the PGA TOUR players go through, travelling from city to city, trying to earn a living. Unlike most professional sports where players are guaranteed an annual salary, golfers get paid only when they perform. If they don't, they still have to pay all their costs associated with travel, lodging, and paying their caddy. I am sure it is a stressful and lonely existence for many.

One day I was playing in a tournament on a really long course nicknamed "Jack's Black". I was struggling to make par and one of the players was Andy Miller, the son of Johnny Miller, U.S. Open Winner, and famous television commentator. Andy was struggling to keep his PGA TOUR card and yet he managed to shoot 9 under par for the day. That day I realized there was still a huge gap between me and the tour players. I was put in my place that day, and I saw how insanely difficult it was going to be to make the top level of professional golf as a member of the PGA TOUR.

I never did qualify for the PGA TOUR, but I did have lots of success at the local level, winning all four Major Championships at my home club of St. Mark Golf Club in Lake San Marcos, California. To this day I am the only golfer ever to do so. I have also had the opportunity to play in many competitive individual and team matches, and I have enjoyed playing recreationally on some of the most scenic courses around the country.

The dream of being a professional golfer never left me, though. When I turned 50, I entered a regional qualifying tournament for the U.S. Senior Open. It was held at Fairbanks Ranch Country Club, and I figured this was the best place to try since I was intimately familiar with the course. I practiced diligently for four months straight and felt I was ready on the day of the event. I played a practice round with Tag Merritt the day before and shot 71. I was confident that with a few good breaks the next day I just might be able to pull it off. Qualifying would mean playing in the U.S. Senior Open with all of golf's legends.

My son Tyler was my caddy. I had won many tournaments with him on my bag. I felt confident and nervous at the same time. One hundred, forty-four players entered and only the top two qualified to play in the U.S. Senior Open. The course, which I had played hundreds of times, was set up in PGA fashion with extremely fast greens, long rough and flags that were tucked in challenging positions.

I started poorly, bogeying three of the first four holes. I turned to Tyler and said, "Let's flip the switch and start playing some golf."

I racked up a couple of birdies and had a sensational eagle on the 10th hole that I will never forget. I was right back in it. I gave it a valiant effort but missed making the cut by five shots. Although disappointed I was not one of the top two, I held my head high as I knew I had given it my best effort.

Just recently, I was sharing my golf journey and how I was sponsored by TaylorMade, with my friend Lee Sanudo. Lee is an accomplished golf instructor who has worked extensively with TaylorMade. He marveled and said, "That is the most incredible golf story I have ever heard. You literally have NO idea what you pulled off. Guys can work in golf shops for years and years, and never receive what you did."

I have been a loyal customer of TaylorMade from the beginning. Last year I decided it was time to upgrade to some new clubs. I asked around at our local club for the best way to get a private fitting set up at TaylorMade's Kingdom. They looked at me like, "Are you kidding?" That place is reserved for the PGA pros. They made a few calls to help me and got nowhere fast.

I decided it couldn't hurt to ask, so I sent an email to The Kingdom fitting center with a request. I explained that they had sponsored me back in 2000, and I was getting serious about my game again. My clubs were almost 20 years old, and I wanted to have a private fitting and was willing to pay for it, if necessary.

An hour later I received an e-mail, and I was booked for a fitting. When I went, I received the same royal treatment and again had my own locker set-up and a personalized placard on the range.

TaylorMade knows how to make me feel special

We tested at least 20 different shafts and several styles of club heads until we found what was right for me. I now own the finest clubs anyone can buy. What makes them extra special is they are personally fitted just for me. When I showed up at the club with my new set of clubs, the club pro was dumbfounded. He said, "How did you pull that off?" I smiled and said, "I just asked."

I now play golf for the sheer joy of it. I enjoy playing on the Senior Golf Team for St. Mark Golf Club, competing against other clubs. I have finally put my dream of playing on the PGA Tour aside with absolutely no regrets. I gave it my all for two full years and realized I am simply not good enough. I am totally okay with that. I have the utmost respect for the PGA Tour players and know first-hand how good they really are. I can appreciate what a difficult path each one has had to follow to get where they are.

Most importantly, I can go to my grave with no regrets. I never have to wonder, "What if?" I will never have to say to myself, "I should have tried!" I am totally complete.

———————◇———————

What Insights did I gain from this experience?

The most rewarding things I do in life are often the ones that look like they cannot be done.

Certainly, my goal of becoming a professional golfer looked like it could not be done — and many people reminded me of that. As it turned out, my quest to become a PGA Tour player was one of the most fulfilling times in my life. I was totally alive again, and each day I looked forward to practicing and getting better. I took on a massive challenge with no idea how to accomplish it. I just systematically broke it down and took on one obstacle at a time. Each minor victory would just add more fuel to my burning passion.

Not knowing what lies ahead when setting big goals can really be an advantage.

Had I known all the obstacles I would eventually have to overcome, I might not have set off on the journey, because it would have looked impossible. In the end, I am so glad I decided to pursue this goal.

One of the biggest life lessons I learned was to focus only on the shot I was making.

In golf, I could not dwell on the previous shot, or worry about the next one. In life, I can only have an effect on what I am doing right now. What I did yesterday can never be changed, and what I have in store for tomorrow cannot be done today. Planning is essential, and learning from experience is important, but focusing on the here-and-now is absolutely the most critical element of success.

Once I was clear on my goal, the universe provided everything I needed – in no time at all.

It all started with a clear goal and being willing to ask for help. Within a week of declaring my goal, I had a place to play for free on a championship course. A week later I was personally fitted for tour-quality golf clubs for free. A week later an LPGA TOUR winner took me under her wing and began coaching me. An "angel" gifted me $500 a month for entry fees. My wife, Janice, became my biggest supporter and fan.

Taking the time to pursue what I really wanted in life was a huge gift to me.

Even though I did not reach the PGA Tour, I had an awesome time giving it my all, despite the long odds. I am extremely proud of what I accomplished. Once again, like competing in the IRONMAN Triathlon World Championships, the journey was a huge boost to my personal confidence.

12
THE LIST

The List
(Artist: Ben Humbert)

"Show me your friends and I will show you your future."

– Anonymous

Back when we still had cassette tapes, I would always have an inspirational or educational tape playing in my car. It was not a fancy car, but it got me around and I used the hours of driving as my personal-growth time.

One day I was listening to a tape in my Mazda 626 and the speaker started talking about the value of the people we associate with. He asked the listeners to write a list of the 10 people we spend the most time with. He suggested that if we were driving, to just make a mental list. These people on our list did not have to be in close proximity, or in daily contact, but they needed to be those we spent the most time with or had the most influence on our life.

While driving, I made my mental list. Of course, it started with my wife, kids, my boss, and my friends. Then he asked a question that forever altered the course of my life.

"Of these ten people on your list, who would you like to model your life around?"

He went on to say that these ten people will either cause us to grow, stay in place or go in reverse. I was stunned. I had to pull over the car and take a deep breath. I was visibly shaking.

I knew that on some level my kids would always inspire me to grow and serve as role models for them, but they were only about eight and five years old at the time. My wife Debbie, although supportive, was happy with the status quo and did not really like change. My boss was not inspiring. None of the friends I had seemed interested in improving themselves, or their situations in life. My parents and brother and sister, who were not on my Top 10 list, lived on the other side of the country, and at that time we were not close.

Basically, I could think of no one on my list other than my kids who were going to help me grow. I was stuck in my life and I realized I was allowing the people on my list to keep me there. I knew things needed to change. Yes, there were people on my list that were nice to me and I enjoyed their company, but they really were not up to much. They were not doing anything I would put in the category of being inspirational.

I decided right then to make some changes. I realized I couldn't write to everyone on the list to tell them they were no longer in my life. That was certainly not my intention. I did, however, become much more conscious of the people I was spending time with and how they made me feel from this new perspective.

I was up for improving my life and taking on new goals. And . . . I saw that the majority of people in my life at that time were not. Just as important, I realized that it was not a supportive relationship for either of us, so I was also helping them by slowly exiting from their lives. Gradually, there was a natural "pulling away" process that took place. Because I had more time for relationships and a different focus, I started attracting new people in my life and others seemed to naturally fade away.

Today, only one person from that original list is still on my top 10 list: my youngest son, Tyler. I am now married to a loving and truly supportive wife who not only shares my goals, but she also cheers me on. I have a great renewed relationship with my brother and his wife, despite the fact that we live thousands of miles away from each other. I am also blessed with numerous business associates and friends who inspire me. This did not happen quickly, but over time people on the list were exchanged for others who inspire me.

Researchers have noticed that when salespeople accustomed to making $25,000 a year moved to an environment where the norm was that everyone was earning more than $100,000 a year, one of two things happened. They either rose to the occasion and started earning more than $100,000 a year, or they were so uncomfortable they quit. They also noticed the same phenomenon occurred when high-income salespeople were in environment where everyone was earning less. Either they lowered their income to fit in, or they became uncomfortable and left.

I concluded that if I wanted to earn more money, I needed to put myself in, or create, an environment where everyone was earning more money. It was that simple. If I wanted to become wealthy, I needed to associate with wealthy people. If I wanted to make a difference in the world, I needed to spend time with people who are up to serving others. If I wanted to be healthy and physically fit, I needed to train with healthy and fit people. The saying, "Birds of a feather, flock together" suddenly took on a whole new meaning. It seems so obvious now, but it was not obvious to me then.

Denzel Washington
(@Success.Portal)

Academy Award winner actor Denzel Washington shared this recently while giving a talk; and it illustrates my point perfectly:

"If you hang around five confident people, you will be the sixth."

"If you hang around five intelligent people you will be the sixth."

"If you hang around five millionaires, you will be the sixth."

"If you hang around five idiots, you will be the sixth."

"BE SMART."

As I became more and more aware of this basic principle, I started to notice it all around me. I observed how many people who suffered from various diseases or addictions seemed to belong to support groups of people with the same challenges. I wondered why they kept being stuck.

Although maybe helpful at first, I deduced that being in a support group with people who suffered the same challenges may only serve to keep them in that support group, beyond the time it was useful or healthy. For example, it's critical for someone with a drug or alcohol problem to associate with people who have never used drugs or alcohol or who have committed to abstaining from them, rather than associating with old friends who currently use these substances. That new environment may cause them to make a shift if they genuinely want to.

As an avid baseball fan, I have seen times when a player not living up to his potential gets traded to a winning team. All of a sudden that player rises to the occasion, and seemingly out of nowhere, his performance dramatically improves. I have also witnessed "star" players, traded to a team that is struggling, not perform to their normal capability.

I also observed a phenomenon that Australians call the "Tall Poppy Syndrome." When applied to people, the term refers to the practice of "cutting down" those experiencing success, by speaking badly of them, sabotaging their work, or implying there is a reason other than merit for their success. I believe this is due to the fact those who are enjoying success (a Tall Poppy) are making others feel inferior. Clearly, however, that is not their intention.

I have seen family situations where one family member wants to leave the nest, get a college education, and make something of themselves. One of two reactions often occur. Either the family is so proud of them and excited for their success they are incredibly supportive of their student, or they do everything they can to sabotage them and keep them in place. The second scenario can create some challenging dynamics where people want to remain loyal to their family, yet don't want to be held back.

While it sure would be nice if the norm were that people were always supportive of other's goals and rooting for their success, I have found that is not always the case. I am not 100% sure, but I suspect it may have something to do with varying levels of self-esteem. When someone close experiences more success than they have, people with lower self-esteem may feel like it is reducing their self-worth.

It takes a big person to be happy for others' success. I remember a time in 1983 when I had just completed my first year of selling life insurance. I earned $56,000 that year and I was so proud. Then I realized I had just surpassed my Dad's annual income as a school principal. It didn't seem fair that I was able to do that in my first year of sales, when he spent his whole life as an educator. It bothered me, and I was reluctant to share my news with him for fear of how he would take it. I eventually did, and I was surprised at his reaction. He was so proud and encouraged me to shoot for the stars. That one interaction changed the direction of my life in a positive way. I can only imagine if he had reacted differently how that would have affected me.

I am so fortunate now to have people in my life who inspired me, and I can count on no matter what. I hope I provide as much inspiration to them as they provide me. The people on my Top 10 List did not happen by accident and the list has taken a long time to develop. I attribute much of my growth to hearing that talk on "The List." It was painful at the time, but so worth it.

Recently I read a quote by the Academy Award-winning actor, Sir Anthony Hopkins that seemed to fit with this chapter.

Sir Anthony Hopkins
(@close-up-blog.blogspot.com)

"Let go of people who aren't ready to love you yet! This is the hardest thing you'll have to do in your life, and it will also be the most important thing. Stop giving your love to those who aren't ready to love you yet. Stop having hard conversations with people who don't want to change. Stop showing up for people who are indifferent to your presence."

What insights did I gain from this experience?

Choosing who I spend time with greatly influences the outcomes in my life.

Spending time with people who inspire me charges my batteries. They help get me fired up, and as a result I can do more with my life. I also believe that if I inspire someone else, they get a positive charge, and everyone benefits.

It is up to me to choose who I spend time with.

It is totally up to me to determine who I want to surround myself with. Having people in my life who are genuinely happy when I experience a win, means the world to me.

13
WHEN OPPORTUNITY KNOCKS

Opening Doors
(Artist: Ben Humbert)

"If someone offers you an amazing opportunity
and you're not sure you can do it, say yes –
then learn how to do it later."

– Sir Richard Branson – founder of the Virgin Group

I t was January of 1995, and I was struggling financially. My wife, Debbie had gone back to Canada and taken our sons with her. My three solid sources of income had all dried up just a couple of months before. I had no income to pay my own bills, much less send child support back to Canada. I was living with Janice in her 385-square-foot studio in the back of someone's house. The situation was bleak, and I felt like I was in a deep hole financially with no ladder to climb out. The rug had been pulled out from beneath me and I was definitely off balance.

I was rebuilding my life with Janice by my side, and we had just finished teaching our first seminar series together. That brought in some much-needed income. It was encouraging, but it was just a drop in the bucket for what I needed to get back on track. I needed a way to generate some income and I needed it fast – but I did not see any options on the horizon. I was in a state of survival, and ready for almost anything.

Sometimes opportunities appear right in front of us and if we are not ready to see them, they pass us by. I was more than ready! I have learned that when opportunity knocks, I have to open the door to take advantage of it.

The San Diego Chargers went to the Super Bowl for the first time ever in January of 1995. They ended up losing but it turned out to be a huge win for me because it became the opportunity I needed. I admit I certainly did not see it coming.

Growing up in Canada, I played football in high school and college, though I was not a huge American football fan. Over the years since I moved to San Diego in 1994, I have come to really appreciate the atmosphere of fun and community that supported our local football team, the Chargers.

It was late afternoon on a Friday in January of 1995 when I had a call from Bill Auger, a former co-worker with me and Janice. He said he had an exciting opportunity and had to meet with me right away. I explained that I was just heading out for dinner with Janice and asked if it could wait until tomorrow. He wondered where we were going and said he would meet us there and just needed 10 minutes of my time. Bill insisted it just could not wait. He seemed so excited, so I said okay. Bill had been working with me and Janice at the Street Smart Business School until we were all laid off just a few months before. I felt obligated to at least hear him out. Bill was a great guy, and he always had a "whatever it takes" attitude. We soon became good friends.

Janice and I went to the restaurant and in came Bill a short while later. He was bubbling over with enthusiasm and could not wait to show us his idea. It revolved around the San Diego Chargers. The previous Sunday, the underdog Chargers had defeated the heavily favored Pittsburgh Steelers in Pittsburgh by the score of 17-13 in the American Football Conference championship game. The Chargers won in one of the most exciting ways possible: they stopped the Steelers on the one-yard line as time ran out at the end of the game.

The Chargers had been in San Diego since 1961 and were going to the Super Bowl for the very first time in their history. The Super Bowl was only nine days away and the city was going completely crazy. I had not been following the team too closely until that week, when the Chargers were all everyone was talking about.

While we sat at dinner, Bill showed us drawings of several items that involved the Chargers. Since the win in Pittsburgh was so unexpected, there was a massive shortage of Chargers gear.

Bill was convinced that if we created these products, we could sell them in no time. The people of San Diego were in a frenzy and he felt they would buy anything they could get their hands on with the Chargers logo.

Bill had several T-shirt designs sketched out, a big foam "number one" mitt that fits over your hand, and a simple yellow pin in the shape of a lightning bolt. I felt the pin was especially promising and that is what we should focus on. It was close enough to the Chargers official logo, but not so much that it would be challenged for copyright infringement. It was made of yellow plastic and was about four-inches long with a simple safety pin on the back. I was immediately drawn to the pin as it was unique and did not have the sizing problems associated with T-shirts, and I felt the big number one foam finger was not original.

I liked his idea and agreed to help him out. Since we had all just been laid off, we could certainly use the extra money. We arranged to meet early the next morning to develop a plan and get into action. We were in a short time window as the Super Bowl was the following Sunday.

I taught in my marketing class that it is important to test-market a product using a small sample size before investing in large-scale production. By doing this we would not be stuck with huge quantities of unsellable items. The last thing we wanted to do was produce thousands of these pins only to find out nobody would buy them. So, we decided to test a small batch of 500. We knew the Carlsbad Marathon was being held the next morning and there were bound to be crowds of people we could test-market to. Even though most people at the race would be runners, not necessarily football fans, at least they would be sports enthusiasts and a good indicator of whether people would buy the pins we created.

Bill had already found a local die cutter and had 500 lightning bolts cut. We still needed the pin to stick on the back. We went to an office supply store and bought hundreds of plastic name tags with a wire pin in the back. We easily removed the pins from the back of each of the name tags. We then went to a craft store and bought a couple of glue guns and glue sticks and went back home and began gluing the pins on the back of our lightning bolts. Once that was done, we bought dark blue hoodies for us to wear, and we pinned a bunch of the yellow lightning bolts all over them. We were sure to be seen.

The next morning, we got up bright and early and began our test-marketing at the race which started at 7:00 a.m. We tried all different pricing strategies and soon found that the best price point was $2.00 each and three for $5.00. Within a few hours we had sold out. One man who had just finished running the marathon decided he had to have some pins. He reached down into his sock and pulled out a very wet $10 bill and bought six. We knew we had a winner and went right into action to go into mass production. We thought big and targeted to sell 20,000 pins.

After creating the initial batch, we found out that the glue did not work so well, so we changed our design and looked for pin backs that had a sticky surface on them. All the craft stores we knew of were already sold out of that type of pin design. I went online and found a company that sold just what we were looking for. I called them and confirmed they could provide us with what we wanted.

They asked me how many "gross" I wanted. I was so green I had no idea what a gross was. I asked the salesperson to, "hold on a second." I looked over at Bill and he told me a gross was 144. I told them we needed 20,000 total which was 139 gross. We made the arrangements to pick them up right away.

Then Bill called the die cutter he used previously to order 20,000 more lightning bolts. Unfortunately, the die cutter only had enough plastic to make about 2,000. We needed to find a supplier for the yellow plastic. We could not find any in San Diego. We finally reached a supplier in Ohio who had the plastic we wanted. We immediately ordered enough material to make 18,000 lightning bolts. Only problem was we needed the material right away and the company was on the other side of the country. The supplier suggested to have it shipped with same-day delivery. I did not even know that could be done. It cost a little more, but with time running out we did not have any other options. Later that day I drove to the San Diego Airport to pick up the shipment as it arrived. I took it straight to the die cutter and he got to work. In the meantime, we started assembling the 2,000 we had and by Monday night we had the rest of the plastic in hand.

This was a new experience for me, and the three of us were definitely flying by the seat of our pants. There was an adrenaline rush that went with it and we just kept moving forward and taking on the next challenge as it arose.

Now we needed to start assembling and selling! We had an extremely limited window of time to get these sold. Once the Super Bowl was over, the market for our lightning bolts would be limited at best, especially if the Chargers lost to the San Francisco 49ers (which they did).

Previously, Janice had made friends with a group of families from Guatemala who lived nearby. She would often drop off used clothing for them. We needed help to assemble all these pins and Janice had a great idea. She asked those families if any of them could help.

Within an hour we had 12 Guatemalans sticking pin backs on to the yellow plastic. We set up a long production table outside in the back yard, put up a heat lamp and Janice made hot soup and sandwiches for everyone. They had mariachi music playing, and everyone was having a grand time.

Our Guatemalan friends were knocking out the pins in no time flat and we put the finished product in plastic Ziploc bags with 50 in a bag. All was going great until about 10:00 that night. The person who was renting the main house that shared the back yard with us was a doctor going through his residency. He had just come home after working 36 hours straight and found this scene in his back yard. Needless to say, he was not happy as he just wanted to crash and get some sleep. So, we turned off the mariachi music and we sent all our Guatemalan friends back home. We had almost all of the pins put together at that point.

While the pins were being produced in our backyard, I called as many people as I knew and asked them if they would like to make a quick and easy thousand dollars. We sold them the pins for a dollar each and then they would sell them for $2.00. The easiest places to sell our pins were gas stations and convenience stores. They would typically start off buying 50 and put them on display at the cash register. Within hours they were calling back asking for more.

One of our friends went into Nordstrom and pitched the product to a manager. They bought 2,000 and were selling them for $4.00 each. Nordstrom is a high-end retail clothing store known for their exceptional quality and service. Our pins looked out of place on a jewelry counter, but they sold out in no time. Getting any product to sell in a store like that typically would take months, along with approval from several levels of decision makers. The fact that one manager was willing to take a risk and put them on their counters was an extraordinary act and a sign of what was going on in the city at that time.

Janice had also met a professional sports-merchandising person at a flea market. He made T-shirts and trinkets for every major sporting event and travelled around the country selling his wares. He decided he wanted to test-market our pins and bought 2,000. I went to his motel room about 10:00 that night with 2,000 pins in plastic bags. I felt like a drug dealer since I was delivering our "product" in baggies. I parked as close to his room as I could and carefully checked my surroundings before getting out of the car. I was scared and nervous about how this transaction was going to go down. I was way out of my comfort zone and asked myself what I was doing there at 10:00 o'clock at night.

I mustered up all my courage, took a deep breath and knocked on his door. He welcomed me in. He was a big burly man who had not shaved in a week and looked like he had not slept for even longer. I suspect he had downed a few beers before I got there. I was stunned by what I saw. His motel room was filled with T-shirts from floor to ceiling with just a narrow path to navigate around his bed. He had T-shirts for both Super Bowl teams. He checked out my goods and pulled out a huge wad of cash from his pocket. He peeled off twenty $100 bills and handed them to me. I put the money in my pocket, quickly ran to my car, and got out of there fast. My heart was pounding as I sped off.

Soon the word was out, and people were showing up at our door at all hours buying baggies of 50 pins to resell.

At night, Janice and I would go out to the bars and sell them there. We would gift the bouncer a pin and ask if we could offer them to the people inside. We would make our rounds and within minutes we would sell at least 50. We also had made a limited supply of small matching dangling earrings to offer. I remember one lady really wanted a pair but did not have any money left so she took off her earrings and traded them for a pair of Charger earrings. As I said earlier, people were so enthused about the Chargers, they would buy anything, and I am sure her earrings cost a whole lot more than what she traded for.

We hardly slept a wink all week. We went around the clock. We took an idea Bill had at 5:00 p.m. on Friday night and just ran with it. None of us had any experience in producing a product like that before. We turned the idea into a small business that generated well over $20,000 in sales in a week. Our production cost for each unit was only 12 cents, so the profit margin was huge.

At the end of the week Bill, Janice and I got together, and we divided up the cash. We sold all but about 200 pins, which we never did sell, as the Chargers have not returned to the Super Bowl – they even left San Diego a few years ago. On that Super Bowl Sunday in 1995, we cheered on the Chargers and even though they lost, we thanked them for the opportunity. Right after the game we went to bed for some much-needed rest.

After it was all over, I reflected on what we had accomplished in that extremely short time span. It was nothing short of miraculous. If we had months to prepare, I doubt we would have been as successful. If we did have the time to set up a proper business, we would need to do all the tasks required to create a company: incorporate a legal entity, come up with a company name, develop a business plan, create a marketing strategy, design a company logo, get business cards printed, etc. Of course, if we took the time to do all that under these circumstances, we would never have sold a single item. We took an idea, saw the opportunity, and ran with it.

––––––––––––––––––––– ♡ –––––––––––––––––––––

What insights did I gain from this experience?

I learned that when opportunity knocks, I have to open the door to take advantage of it.

I realize now that I do not have to have all the details solved or have the knowledge of how everything will work out in order to start something new. The learning occurs once I make the decision to move forward.

Time frames, and other obstacles that seem impossible to solve, become almost irrelevant when I combine enthusiasm with a sense of urgency and commitment.

Never once during the week did we ever question our decision to do this. We faced many obstacles that we had not anticipated. We just took each one head-on as it came up and solutions seemed to come from nowhere. Had we wavered in our commitment in any way, the whole project would have either been dropped or delayed so much we would have missed the opportunity.

14
PEPPERDINE

**With Tyler on the Pepperdine University Campus
overlooking Malibu – 2003**

*"Your present circumstances don't determine where you
go; they merely determine where you start."*

– Dr. Nido R. Qubein,
President of High Point University

It was several years after my divorce before my parents would even talk to me. I felt shunned by my family. I was also hurt they did not warm up to Janice. They thought she was the "Wicked Witch of the West" who caused my marriage to break up. That was the farthest thing from the truth, but it was their reality and what they believed. They skipped our wedding, which was really painful to both Janice and me.

About eight years into our marriage, I decided to turn that relationship around. I called my parents and told them I would like to fly them from Ottawa to San Diego to visit us. I have made a lot of sales calls in my life, but this was definitely one of the hardest calls for me to make. I was really afraid they would say no. After a few days they agreed, so we picked the date, and I went online to find the best rates for a trip with the most direct route. I found a flight on Northwest Airlines and even though we had already agreed on the dates, I called my Dad to confirm before I purchased the tickets.

I gave him all the details and he said the dates were fine, but my Dad had a bad experience with Northwest Airlines and asked if I could find another airline. I bit my tongue and went back to searching for another flight. This was when we still had a dial-up modem and did not have all the travel websites we have today, so it was quite tedious looking at all the alternatives.

I eventually found a flight on Delta that transferred planes in Atlanta. My father agreed to it and so I booked it. That was the first of many "coincidences" that led to my son Tyler attending Pepperdine University.

My parents were already seated after they changed planes in Atlanta when this towering African-American man wearing a New York Knicks warm-up jersey and hat came to sit beside Mom and Dad. My Dad was 6'3, weighed 240 pounds, and wore size 13 EE wide shoes. As he looked down at this stranger's feet, they were even bigger. My Dad was a former athlete and recognized another athlete when he saw one.

Because the man was wearing a Knicks jersey my Dad asked, "Do you play basketball?" The man said he had and introduced himself as Embry Malone. He was now a coach and scout, and he had a team playing in the Summer Pro League tournament at Cal State University in Long Beach. He shared with my Dad that the Summer Pro League is an annual event where the top college and semi-pro players from the U.S. and Europe come to be scouted by NBA teams.

The two of them hit it off and talked basketball all the way to San Diego. When they departed, he gave my Dad his hat and jersey and told him to come to Irvine to catch a couple of games. He gave him his number and told my Dad to call, and he would have complimentary tickets waiting for him at Will Call.

My Dad was so excited. My sons Graham and Tyler were already with us for the summer. Graham had finished high school and Tyler was about to enter his senior year. Both played basketball in high school and Tyler really loved it. They wanted to go to the game as well, so my Dad got on the phone to see if he could get tickets for all of us. Either he had the wrong number, or Embry was not picking up his phone. My Dad was a stubborn man and kept trying to reach him.

Finally, I said to my Dad, "Why don't we just go? The tickets can't be that much." We agreed and that afternoon we all piled into the car and drove to The Walter Pyramid at Cal State University, Long Beach. The Pyramid is a landmark structure. There are only three true pyramids built in the United States. This one stands 18 stories high and the whole exterior is a striking cobalt blue, which can be seen from virtually everywhere on campus. It has a seating capacity of 5,000 for basketball games.

The Walter Pyramid – Cal State University, Long Beach

We bought our tickets and headed inside to watch one of the games. The players' ability was extremely high caliber. We instantly recognized the coach on one of the teams: Kareem Abdul Jabbar. There were scouts everywhere.

My Dad was still hell bent on finding Embry. He finally happened upon his personal assistant who called him at his hotel, and he came over to meet us. By now it was almost 9:00 p.m. I will never forget meeting Embry. Tyler was by my side and Embry asked him if he was "a baller." Tyler replied "Yes." Then he asked him if he was a "Dud or a Stud?" Tyler did not know what to say. Then Embry asked if he was a "Hero or a Zero?" How does a young skinny teenager from a small high school in Canada answer that question coming from a huge man who is a scout and coach? Finally, Embry asked Tyler if he brought a highlight video he could watch.

Now to put everything in perspective, Tyler played on a team in a small high school in a rural area outside of Ottawa, Canada. I suspect everyone who came to the first practice made the team. It is extremely unlikely there will ever be a graduate from that high school who makes the NBA or gets a scholarship to play on a Division 1 U.S. university basketball team. Having a highlight video was never a thought. Even if it was, it is unlikely any of his games were video-taped. So of course, he answered, "No – I don't have one." Embry then asked Tyler what he was doing at 8:00 a.m. the next morning. Tyler was on summer vacation so did not have any plans. Embry then shocked us and invited Tyler to come and work out with his team the next morning. Then he said, "I will tell you if you are a Dud or a Stud, and if you are a Hero or a Zero – see you at eight o'clock."

By then it was 10:00 p.m. and all of Tyler's gear was miles away in San Diego so we got in the car to head back. The drive at night with no traffic was just over an hour and I knew that if we wanted to arrive at Long Beach by 8:00 a.m. we were going to hit morning rush-hour traffic. We would have to leave by 5:45 a.m. to be safe. I am sure Tyler did not sleep a wink that night. Tyler had not touched a basketball in months so wanted to get there a little early to shoot around. So, we left at 5:30 and beat all the traffic. We arrived at the imposing Pyramid by 6:45 a.m. The place was deserted. The doors were locked.

Tyler and I walked all around the building and found a door at the back that was unlocked, and we went in. Naturally, the gym was in darkness and no one was around at that time. We stumbled across a caretaker who asked what we were doing and how we got in. After we explained why were there, he was truly kind and turned on the lights for us and gave us a ball. That was a special moment for me, and I am sure it was for Tyler, too. To shoot hoops in the Pyramid all alone at 7:00 a.m. is truly a magical experience.

Tyler's high-school gym would probably seat about 100 people and was poorly lit. The Pyramid was a whole different experience. The ceiling is almost 200 feet high, and the lighting is incredible. The caretaker had turned on the lights just over the floor and the 5,000 seats were in darkness. It felt like we were in a movie with a spotlight shining on us. If that were the end of the story, I would still be happy, however as they say in the infomercials: "But wait ... there's more!"

At 8:00 a.m., Embry and his team came in. He told Tyler to just jump in with the team and go through the drills. Embry did not really introduce Tyler to the team and just told them he was going to work out with them today. Tyler was still a growing boy and was dwarfed by these much older players who obviously had spent a lot of time both playing basketball and working out in the weight room. The team was made up of top college players with a couple of guys who played professional basketball in Europe. One was 7 feet tall.

Tyler showed up big that day. I was so proud of him. He was as fast and as agile as the rest of them and seemed like he belonged. As couple of times during the practice Embry looked over at me and gave me the thumbs up. An hour later, practice was over, and Embry came over to talk to us. He said Tyler had lots of potential and invited him to come back next summer and play on his team.

Then he asked Tyler what his plans for university were. Tyler didn't have any plans, so Embry suggested he go to Pepperdine. That is where he had gone to school and played on the same team as NBA Legend, Dennis Johnson. Embry started out at Pepperdine as a "walk-on" – which meant he had no scholarship – made the team and earned his scholarship later. Embry said he could arrange for an interview with the Head Coach, Paul Westphal – a former NBA player who is now in the Hall of Fame. Embry suggested that Tyler apply to the university soon, as he had to get accepted first before he could receive a basketball scholarship or even try out for the team.

Was Tyler ready at that time to play for a Division 1 basketball team at Pepperdine? Looking back, I would have to honestly say I did not think so, but that never stopped any of us.

The next step was to go to Pepperdine to check it out. Pepperdine is in Malibu, California, perched high on a hill overlooking the Pacific Ocean. Growing up in Canada I had watched many college sporting events on TV and they always showcased how beautiful a campus it was. The views are stunning, and a far cry from the high school Tyler was attending. In my wildest dreams, I never thought my son would be able to attend such a prestigious university. It was almost like being in a fairy tale, but since we were living it, and all these "coincidences" kept lining up, I decided to just go with it.

We stayed in touch with Embry all summer. He was having a hard time reaching Coach Westphal, so we decided to visit the school to check it out. I called the university and they arranged for us to go on a guided tour on a Friday morning at the end of August. The night before, they called to say our tour leader was sick and rescheduled us for Monday (which happened to be the first day of school). That change in plan turned out to be another great "coincidence."

We arrived at the campus and we were greeted by deer grazing on the lush green grass by the Pepperdine University sign. We went on the tour and were stunned by the beauty of the campus. Tyler also noticed the California girls were nice-looking. We had lunch in the cafeteria, and as we were reading the school brochure, we saw the tuition was $40,000. Tyler thought that was rather good for four years. Too bad it was for just one year – and room and board weren't even included!

After we finished with the educational part of the tour, we decided to make our way to the gym and see if we could track down Coach Westphal. We found the basketball court and there was one person there shooting hoops. Tyler and I looked at each either and said, "Isn't that Reggie Miller?" Reggie is an NBA legend and one of the best shooters ever to play the game. We were mesmerized. We watched him for at least 20 minutes, and it seemed like he never missed. What an experience.

After a while, we went back on our mission to find Coach Westphal. We asked around and got directed to his office. Fortunately, he was there. We poked our head in the door and he introduced himself. He welcomed us in. He acknowledged that Embry had been trying to reach him, but he had been in Europe all summer recruiting and just got back the day before. Another coincidence? If that tour guide had not been sick on Friday, we would have never met Coach Westphal.

We sat down with him for at least an hour, and he answered all our questions. Here Tyler amazed me. We were sitting in front of a basketball legend, yet he seemed completely unfazed by his presence. Tyler spoke up and asked him directly "So, Coach, what do I need to do to make the team?" I was stunned by my son's boldness and confidence.

Coach said they carry 15 players on the team. Twelve get full scholarships. Three were "walk-ons" and at the end of the first year, if they have performed well, they would likely get a scholarship the following year. Tyler then asked how many players typically tried out for those three spots. Coach answered "Twelve". We did the math and figured those were good odds. First, he had to get accepted, then show up to practice and take his chances.

Janice and I agreed to pay Tyler's first year of tuition if he got accepted and then it was up to him to get a scholarship.

Tyler went back to Ottawa the next week and worked at improving his grades. He submitted his application to attend the prestigious Pepperdine University. Months later he called me in California to say he was accepted. I will never forget that day. I was so happy for him and so proud.

Thank goodness my Dad had a bad experience with Northwest Airlines, or none of this would have happened!

Of course, coincidences like these happen to us all the time, but at each turn along the way we have a decision to seize the opportunity or not. Tyler chose to accept and never looked back.

Tyler attended Pepperdine for a year, which was a huge learning experience. He went to the first team practice only to find that all 15 spots for the team were already taken. The assistant coach told them that unless he was the next "Michael Jordan" he would not be making the team. It was a big let-down for Tyler. He was invited to scrimmage with the women's team, as they needed outside players to scrimmage against, but it just was not the same.

Tyler enjoyed the university life and soon was dating a good-looking girl who was the daughter of a famous reality TV star. That summer they invited him to tutor their younger son while travelling on the French Riviera on their yacht. That was an introduction to a completely different world and lifestyle.

As there was little chance of playing basketball at Pepperdine, and because the tuition was so steep, Tyler transferred in his second year to Palomar College – a community college in San Marcos, CA, near where we lived. He played for the Palomar Comets for two years under the guidance of Coach John O'Neill who was a great teacher with high integrity. He was always teaching life lessons that often had little to do with basketball. I remember one day, Coach O'Neill came to practice and announced that one of the players was no longer with the team. We never found out why, but he said the team was going to experience "addition by subtraction." The team instantly became stronger and ended up being Conference Champions.

Tyler playing at Palomar College, 2006

I was fortunate to be their bench coach, so I got to see all his games up close and personal. Janice became their nutrition coach and before every road game we packed lunches for all the players. Many of the players had little money for food and were living away from home, so they really appreciated it.

Tyler's grades continued to improve, and he maintained a perfect 4.0 GPA. He was later recruited by Roberts Wesleyan College in Rochester, New York where he played ball and finished his teacher's degree. He earned a partial athletic scholarship and was awarded several academic scholarships there as well.

Tyler did not make the team at Pepperdine, but the experience was invaluable and set the foundation for many great things in his life. Tyler's basketball career continued, as he coached the freshman and junior teams at Carlsbad High School for three years so he could give back. His teams won their conference every year and he continued teaching his players life lessons. It was an honor to go to his games and see the respect his players had for him. Their parents loved him, too. Tyler still plays basketball several times a week in a recreational league, and his team keeps racking up championships.

None of this story would have happened if my Dad did not ask me to change his flight.

Most importantly, none of this would have happened if Tyler did not seize every opportunity presented to him along the way. He has quietly, and with the utmost of determination, taken advantage of every favorable circumstance given to him and he has made the most of them. When the situations were not right, he made new ones.

After graduating from Roberts Wesleyan College with his teaching degree, Tyler realized teaching was not the career path for him. He decided to create a new "circumstance" in his life and joined The Davidson Group Realty, just a week after graduation.

It was a humble beginning. He started by helping us prepare properties for sale by painting, landscaping, moving furniture, and doing general handyman work. After a solid year of apprentice work, he decided to get his license and start selling real estate. He has never looked back. He consistently surpasses his lofty sales goals and has earned the respect of his peers and all his clients. In 2017, Tyler earned his Brokers License and now plays an integral role in the success of the company.

I am so proud of his accomplishments, and even more of the man and the leader he has become.

Tyler Davidson, Broker Associate of The Davidson Group Realty
(Jill Jones Photography)

What insights did I gain from this experience?

Opportunities are presented to us all the time - often when we least expect them.

I learned that I always need to be aware and open to new possibilities as they arise. What I do with the opportunities determines the path of my life. It takes great courage to forge new paths and take risks.

I have learned to pay great attention to what are referred to as "coincidences."

Coincidences are just road signs telling me which path to follow. They are presented to me all the time, and I have learned to trust my gut as to which path to follow. Sometimes that path is a complete 180-degree turn from where I'm currently headed.

I have learned not to listen to other people's opinions as to what is realistic.

Tyler chose to pursue a goal of playing Division 1 basketball at Pepperdine University. Given his circumstances at the time, most people agreed that was not a realistic goal. He did not achieve his goal, but had he not gone for it he would have lost so many other opportunities in life. That one decision led him on a path that no one could predict where it would lead. Turns out, it was an excellent decision. I applaud Tyler's courage and tenacity for striving to be the best and never giving up.

I realized that it is never too late to rebuild relationships with those close to us.

It took great courage to pick up the phone and invite my parents to visit us after there was such a strain in our relationship. It could have gone either way. I am grateful they accepted the invitation.

15

THE BIRTH OF THE DAVIDSON GROUP REALTY

The Team at The Davidson Group Realty
Left to Right: Tyler Davidson, Jason Daniels,
Janice Davidson, Doug Davidson, and Ben Humbert.
November 2020, Lake San Marcos, CA
(Matt Marshall Photography)

When people ask, "What Do You Do?"
tell them, "Whatever It Takes"

– Anonymous

I called a Realtor to ask a follow up question on a home for sale at $13,000,000. She never, ever returned my phone call. I was dumfounded. The commission for her would have been $325,000.

Janice and I toured a home for sale in Fairbanks Ranch, CA in 1999 with our friends Mark and Bridget Wright. It was called Eagles Nest. This was without a doubt the most exquisite home I had ever been in. It was more than 17,000 square feet and perched high on a hill. The massive picture windows took full advantage of the views of The Del Mar Racetrack, The Del Mar Country Club, The Fairbanks Ranch Country Club, and the Pacific Ocean off in the distance. The home was worth every penny of the asking price.

The quality of craftsmanship was off the charts. I have never been in a home so large, and so elegant that still felt like a comfortable home. Many of the large homes I have seen feel more like museums than a place where you can relax. The furnishings alone in this home were worth $3,000,000. I could have moved in right away – all I needed was my toothbrush.

We were not in a financial position to buy it, but the Realtor didn't know that. Not only did she potentially lose out on a huge commission, but she also was not acting in the best interest of her seller.

Eventually, she lost the listing and another Realtor ended up selling it a year later. That one lesson of the importance of returning phone calls stuck with me forever.

This happened during the time I was teaching my marketing course and I often used that experience as an example of what not to do in business, as I stressed the importance of following up with clients. I remember declaring to the class that if I ever came back in another lifetime, I would come back as a Realtor, as it would be so easy to set myself apart from the competition.

In 2002, Janice and I had been married for four years. We were living in La Costa in the North County of San Diego. Our business was doing well and we decided it was time to stop renting and buy a house. We settled on living in Lake San Marcos, a beautiful suburb nestled up against the mountains and far enough away from downtown so there was wildlife and traffic was manageable. It is an extraordinary community made up of single-level homes, and includes two golf courses, a lake, tennis, swimming pools, a hotel, and fine dining overlooking the water. Best of all, it is quiet.

As we started looking, our experience dealing with Realtors was dreadful. None of them treated selling real estate like a proper business. It was more of a hobby for them. Few returned our phone calls or showed up on time for appointments.

I remember going to one Open House and the Realtor was slouched over in his chair, snoring loudly. We toured the home, left, and he never woke up. Needless to say we didn't buy that one. We went to a different house where there was a big blue tarp on the roof and an aluminum bucket in the middle of the floor catching the rain drops. Not a good look. Another one had a junk-yard dog in the living room growling at us. The Realtor said, "Don't worry. He's friendly." We avoided that room and moved on to the next house.

In general, my experience with Realtors and their level of professionalism left me underwhelmed. Sadly, not much has changed in the industry since then. I might even venture to say it has become worse. My contract as the Golf Operations Manager at Fairbanks Ranch had ended by that point, so I was looking to fill the void in my working life. I was still practicing my golf almost daily. Janice suggested that I get my real-estate license so I could combine meeting people on the golf course while earning a good living. As always, she has the best ideas – and I pursued getting my license.

I soon was completely disenchanted with the industry and saw a real need I could fill. I set out to raise the bar and create a level of service that was unparalleled.

When I received my license in 2003, I sent out an announcement letter to all my acquaintances to let them know of my new venture. I got off to a quick start and sold more than $8,000,000 of real estate in my first year. At the time I was still golfing competitively and was practicing almost daily. My golfing buddies would ask for advice on real estate and refer me to their friends. Many of them and their friends are still buying and selling with me as their chosen Realtor to this day.

My parents taught me the importance of giving first with no expectation of anything in return. I completely endorse that value and practice it regularly. Since I had played in many golf tournaments, I recognized how many volunteers it takes to organize and put one on. I thought a great way to give back to the sport would be a volunteer myself. I approached the President of the Board for the Men's Club at Lake San Marcos Country Club (since renamed as St. Mark Golf Club). I volunteered and was put in charge of organizing the tournaments. I served five years as a volunteer and eventually became President myself.

A few months after I started volunteering there, I received a call from the President of the Men's Club on a Saturday morning. He asked me to meet him at his home, as he wanted to discuss something privately and did not want to do it at the Club. I thought maybe I had done something wrong with the last tournament and it felt like I was being called in to the principal's office.

Much to my relief – and my surprise – when I got there, he said that he had just put an offer in to buy a home at the Pauma Valley Country Club and he wanted me to sell his home in Lake San Marcos. I was surprised he did not use the Realtor that helped him buy his home just a few years earlier and asked him why. He explained how he had been watching the way I conducted my business and wanted to give me a chance. The only caveat was that his home had to be sold quickly, as he needed the money to buy his next home.

He gave me a tour of his home and asked when we could get started. I told him I could go home right then and get a sign to put on his front yard, but I felt that would be a mistake. I told him we only have one chance to make a first impression and suggested that with a few modifications we could dramatically improve the curb appeal. That all-important first impression would ultimately result in a faster sale, for more money.

He had one of the best golf-course locations and a very desirable three-bedroom, two-bath home. We then did another tour of his home and I made some suggestions. The front yard of his home did not have any grass and the "rock lawn" was off-white. The house itself was all one color, also an off-white. There was no trim color to give it any pop. The coach lamps by the garage were the original brass lanterns and they were pitted and looked worn. Same thing with the brass house numbers. There were no flowers to add any color. The inside looked good, except for the kitchen. The cabinets were painted white and were chipped all around the edges and the cabinet knobs and handles were dated.

I suggested that we have the kitchen cabinets painted, replace the knobs and handles, replace the outside lights and numbers with ones that were more current, purchase shutters for the front windows, paint them a contrasting color, and paint the front door the same color. Finally, I suggested we add two big pots with bright red geraniums to put by the front door. He loved the ideas but was worried we did not have much time to get this all done as he really needed it sold by the following weekend.

I called a painter I had used before, but he was not available for the next two weeks. Since we were on a tight time crunch, I did something that altered the course of my real-estate business forever. I told him I had put myself through university by painting homes in the summer and said I would be willing to paint the kitchen cabinets and take care of all the exterior work if he was comfortable with that. I was prepared to do "whatever it takes" to get this sold quickly for him.

He agreed and we immediately drove to Home Depot and picked up the lights, numbers, shutters, a nice green paint for the exterior trim, white paint for the cabinets, hardware for 47 cabinets, two big pots, planting soil, and flowers.

I got to work that afternoon. As I finished painting the cabinets, he installed the hardware. By Wednesday, everything was complete, and the transformation was incredible. The total expense to the seller for materials was less than $500.

I then installed the sign and began marketing the home. We did our first Open House on Saturday afternoon. Many of the curious neighbors had to stop in to check out what I had done. They had watched me working outside for the past several days and I created quite a buzz on the street. No one had ever witnessed a Realtor doing this before.

Towards the end of the Open House, the Realtor who originally sold them the house five years earlier showed up with some clients and they wrote a full-price offer that day. Naturally, the seller was thrilled. He has referred me to several people since and still does to this day, 17 years later. I started tracking the sales that came directly or indirectly from the sale of that home and stopped keeping track after 13 sales. I have since sold that home again when the buyers moved to Texas.

Another investor who bought homes, fixed them up and resold them, (commonly known as a "flipper") lived just down the street. He saw how quickly I had sold this home and gave me a chance to sell one of his homes a few doors down. I eventually sold three homes for him. Our company has already sold 61 homes on that street alone out of a total of 311. We have sold one of them four times!

I am forever grateful that my client, and now friend, from the golf club, gave me a chance to sell his home. I realize what a big risk it was for him and I did not take that responsibility lightly.

A few years after starting in real estate, I got my Broker's License and formed The Davidson Group Realty. I was soon joined by my wife Janice and son Tyler, who was 24 at the time. Tyler now has his Broker's License and is taking on more responsibility in the company.

Over the years I added more Realtors, and one year, our team grew from 6 to 12 in a matter of months. It was so exhilarating to see such rapid growth. However, I soon found a team that size was difficult to manage and not as effective. Not everybody was on the same page. Some were making it a full-time business and giving it 100%, while others were treating it as a part-time venture. I likened it to a sports team I played on in college where not everybody was pulling their weight. That scenario created problems in the locker room, and it caused problems in my office, too, as the synergy that comes from a well-focused team was not there.

I had created this situation and I knew I had to come up with a solution that would work for everyone involved. As a business owner, the hardest thing I have to do is to let someone go. I feel somewhat responsible for each person's livelihood and genuinely want to see each team member be successful. But when the team was not working effectively, I felt things had to change. I spent hours discussing this with Janice and many sleepless nights deciding what to do. Eventually I made the decision to let some people go while some just naturally faded away. Those were some tough decisions to make and were even harder to implement.

In the end, I feel that it was best for all. Some of the people I let go are thriving with other companies and I am happy for them.

Others were simply not a good fit for real estate and never succeeded in this business after leaving our office. As a result of all these moves, we now have a core group of five (pictured in the photo above) who work together like a well-oiled machine. Everyone pulls their weight and supports each other. The synergy is perfect.

To this day, 18 years later, we still go through an extensive preparation process with every home we sell. Only one in 20 homes need little, if anything, to prepare it for sale. The rest need a combination of minor repairs, landscaping, painting, carpet cleaning or replacement, repairs, termite work, decluttering, and staging. We never put a home on the market until it is "show ready." Because of our extensive experience and commitment to excellence, we sell our homes faster and for more money than any of our competitors. In 2020, our average time on the market was 10.9 days (even in the middle of the COVID-19 crisis). The industry average was 34 days.

Due to our full-service customer focus and our insistence that every home we sell be as perfect as it can be, our success has been astounding. In 2020, we sold just shy of 100 homes, totaling almost $60,000,000 in sales.

Our average sales price compared to our listing price is 99.5% compared to the industry average of 96.4%. That 3.1 % difference in the net amount our clients receive pays for our commission, so in essence we work for them for free. And the time we save them selling their home means less money they need to spend on mortgage payments, taxes, utilities, and HOA payments, to say nothing of the saved aggravation of having to show their home over and over, and always needing to keep it clean and show-ready.

With these results, there is no surprise as to why we keep getting referrals. In fact, our marketing strategy is simple. We create a big enough "wow-factor" that our clients keep referring us. Obviously, it takes a great deal more energy to do what we do. However, in 18 years I have never purchased one internet lead or made a single cold call. I know many Realtors who spend 90% of their time on the phone dialing for dollars.

All of our success stems from one basic principle: be willing to do whatever it takes to get the job done.

We also do all the little things right that add up in a big way. Our voicemail says we will return phone calls within the hour, and we consistently honor that commitment. We show up for appointments on time. All of our signage, business cards, and branding is professional and congruent. We take extra care with all the paperwork involved in a transaction and ensure everything is done in a timely manner. These seem like basic fundamentals, but by doing them all, it sets us apart from everyone else in the industry.

Over the years we have developed an incredible team of contractors we can count on and they all share our philosophy. Our extremely talented and widely varied team includes painters, landscapers, the best carpet cleaner ever, flooring installers, a window washer who absolutely loves his job, a "jack of all trades" handyman, electrician, plumber, termite inspector, appraiser, an awesome mortgage broker, and the most dedicated team of escrow and title officers you could ask for.

We also started staging properties long before staging became a thing. In addition to being a superb Realtor, my wife Janice still does all the staging for our company. We call her the Queen of Staging as she does it better than anyone else out there. She has an incredible eye and can see an empty room and transform it. Or, if we already have furniture in place belonging to the seller, she moves it around and completely shifts the energy, thereby creating a harmonious, beautiful, and welcoming atmosphere. She has studied Feng Shui, the Chinese "Art of Placement," to maximize "Chi" or energy. She is truly a master at it.

Now that we have this team of great trades people, I don't paint rooms much anymore, as my time is better spent selling homes. But whenever the occasion arises where something needs to be done quickly, I am always the first to jump in. It is not uncommon to see me planting flowers in front of a house to put the finishing touches on it.

We also have developed a unique culture within our company. Most of the big-box realty companies have a culture where everyone is competing against each other in the office. Instead, we come from a place of cooperation. We work together to get things done and cheer each other on. When a home needs to be staged, we rent a truck and the team descends on the home and carries all the furniture in and is placed where Janice wants it. Sometimes it is moved three or four times before it is right. We get just as excited when another team member sells a home as we do when we sell one of our own homes. It is an exceedingly rare dynamic and a joy to be part of.

Another philosophy we believe in is the Win-Win-Win concept. Most Realtors practice the Win-Lose philosophy. They try to have their client win, often at the expense of someone else. We believe, and practice daily, that a transaction must be a win for everyone sitting at the table. That includes the buyer and seller, the Realtors, the escrow company, title company, lender and all the tradespeople involved in the transaction. If it is not a win for everyone, we choose not to participate.

I have turned down a lot of business from people who play the Win-Lose game. Recently I had a call from an individual who wanted to invest in a number of rental-income properties. I asked him what type of property he was looking for. When he said it did not matter, he just wanted anything he could get for a steal. I told him I did not work that way and politely declined to work with him. I gave up some commission but maintained my integrity.

I am so proud of what we have put together and the level of service The Davidson Group Realty continues to provide. I never take for granted what we do. For us, it is way more than selling homes. We are very aware that each situation is different. We might be serving a first-time home buyer, working with a seasoned investor, selling a home for an estate where someone has died, liquidating a home because of a divorce or a bad financial situation, assisting an elderly person sell their home and move into a retirement home, or helping someone move up to their Dream Home. Each scenario triggers different emotions within our clients. They could be feeling fear, excitement, mourning, sadness, greed, or nervousness. Combine all these intense emotions with large sums of money and it can be a recipe for some atypical behavior. We have learned to be exceptionally good listeners, cheer-leaders, arbitrators, negotiators and on occasion marriage counsellors.

Another service we provide has helped both our clients and the veteran community as well. Most times when people move out of a home, they have furniture they no longer want or will not fit in their new location. In the case of a trust sale, everything must go. We have discovered there are countless veterans living in completely empty apartments. They have gone from being homeless, to finally getting an apartment where it takes every resource they can muster, just to pay the rent. For example, we have had calls through our networks that a veteran needs a bed. We find a good one (or buy one if we need to) and personally deliver it to their door. When we see an empty place, we step up.

In the last few years, we have completely furnished at least 15 homes for deserving veterans. The veterans are typically way too proud to ask for help. They often see asking for assistance as a sign of weakness. I remember in particular one young Marine who needed help. His family had been defending America since the Civil War and he was so proud of his heritage. We heard he had just secured his apartment but needed a separate fully furnished bedroom for his five-year-old daughter in order to have visitation rights as part of his divorce agreement. The case worker was coming the following week and he really needed help. We found out that his place was nearly empty. All he had was a television on the floor, an air mattress in his bedroom, a coffee pot, and his service dog. That was it. His clothes were on the floor, as he did not have any hangers.

The weekend before the case worker's visit, we showed up with a 20-foot U-Haul truck complete with a bedroom set for his daughter. We also had dolls and toys for her, a new bed and dresser for his room, a round dining room table with four chairs, a couch and matching chair, dishes, pots and pans, cutlery, and a weeks' worth of groceries. It was like Christmas in July. He was speechless. We found out after the social worker's visit that he was granted permission for his daughter to stay with him. I could share countless stories like this. It is great to be able to repurpose items in this wonderful way.

We don't do this type of volunteer work for any reason other than to give back, and it gives us joy. In October of 2017, Janice and I were presented with the State of California, Senate Certificate of Recognition as California Heroes of the Month. This was quite an honor to be recognized for our work with veterans.

**Receiving the Senate Certification of Recognition
from Senator Joel Anderson**

Ten years ago, my son Tyler came up with a trademarked tag line for our business that honestly says it all.

"We do more than sell homes, we make a difference!"

———————◇———————

What insights did I gain from this experience?

I learned that the willingness to do whatever it takes to help our clients is a fundamental key to success.

This attitude is part of everything we do. Many things we do are not expected of a typical Realtor and are certainly not on the real-estate licensing exam. Here is a small sample of this week's activities: driving an elderly client to the bank to get a cashier's check, shipping items inadvertently left behind to a new home on the other side of the country, helping a seller find a short-term rental so they can move out on time, delivering boxes to a seller's home so they can pack, and in the case of a trust sale, completely disposing or selling every item in the home so we can then begin to start to do our job of selling the home. Every week is different, and we take it all on with the same attitude. Going the extra mile for clients pays big dividends in the long run.

Taking the extra time at the beginning to prepare a home for sale will generate massive results in the end, and in a much shorter time frame.

As I shared above, preparing a home for sale the right way produces huge results. It requires a lot more work for us in the beginning, but means the sale happens faster and makes more money for our clients and everyone is happy. This lesson of preparing ahead of time applies to many successes in my life.

Cooperating as a small team will always outperform a large group competing against each other.

There is a synergy that comes from cooperation. When people are competing against each other there is no synergy. Worse, that environment can be a damaging energy for all.

Giving first, and giving back to those in need, is extremely rewarding.

As our slogan says, "We do more than sell homes, we make a difference!" There is nothing more gratifying than to be able to help others who are in need.

Finding the right people for the job is crucial, and not everyone is a perfect fit.

Sometimes people are just in the wrong place and not inspired. When that situation occurs, it is best for the company, and ultimately best for them, that they find a different company or career.

16

THE POWER OF
ACKNOWLEDGEMENT

Bridget and Mark Wright

"No one who achieves success does so without acknowledging the help of others. The wise and confident acknowledge this help with gratitude."

– Alfred North Whitehead -
British mathematician and philosopher.

"Doug, I don't know what to do. Bridget had a terrible accident. She is in the hospital and the doctors are trying to determine if she is going to need surgery. She is hanging by a thread and one wrong move could mean the difference between life and death."

Two years ago, in 2018, I experienced firsthand, the "Power of Acknowledgement" in a way that was extremely impactful.

It happened when I received that unexpected call from my good friend and mentor, Mark Wright. I could tell right away he was totally distraught. He let me know that his wife Bridget had a serious accident while riding her bike. She had fallen and broken a vertebra in her neck. She was in the hospital and the doctors were trying to determine the best course of action.

After receiving the call from Mark, I immediately booked the next available flight from San Diego to the Lake Tahoe area where they were living. Mark was in complete overwhelm with the severity of Bridget's injury and needed a friend. I am so grateful I was able to be there for him during this extremely stressful time.

Mark is one of the best business coaches on the planet and he is an absolute master at many things, but technology and cooking are not high on his skills list. Those are things Bridget handles, which allows Mark to do what he does best.

Soon after I arrived, Mark handed me his cell phone and Bridget's cell phone and asked if I would respond to the text messages that had come in. He was not really sure how text messages worked and wanted to keep their friends informed. I was totally stunned at what I saw. In the first 24 hours since her accident at least 50 people had emailed, texted, or called to find out how Bridget was doing. The outpouring of love and genuine concern for Bridget was really overwhelming. Messages were coming in from all over the country. Somehow the word was out, and it spread quickly. I took the time to respond to each and every person and did my best to do it in a way that would honor Bridget's way of communicating. It was almost impossible to keep up with the flood of heartfelt messages coming in.

Eventually I had to start a group text and email list and would update everyone daily with her progress. That allowed me time to do what I could to support Mark and Bridget. I stayed there for ten days until Bridget had her surgery and was able to come home. I was made aware that prayer groups were set up all over the country for Bridget. Her friends near where she lived set up a food-delivery program, and each day, they would drop off meals. The meals were ready to be served and just needed to be warmed. When I left, I knew Mark and Bridget were in good hands.

If ever there was a person who should earn the "Queen of Acknowledgment Award" it would go, hands down, to Bridget Wright. She is a master at making everyone feel they are the most important person in the world to her. She always has time for a call and anytime something noteworthy happens in my life there is always a card in the mail. It could be a birthday card, congratulations, anniversary, thank-you or whatever the occasion is. But what sets her cards apart from others I receive, is the time she takes to write a personal note that is always from her heart. In short, Bridget is an incredible human being with an outpouring of love and generosity that is hard to match.

On the flight home I reflected on my experiences and wondered how this woman had developed such powerful friendships with people all around the country. They genuinely loved her. I am certain that a huge reason is the way she takes the time to communicate with each person in a special way and how she acknowledges them with her sincerity.

I learned a great deal about the value of acknowledging and communicating with special friends from Bridget and Mark that week and am forever grateful for their friendship. I am happy to report that Bridget has made a full recovery.

Back in 1986, I attended a course called *The Power of Acknowledgement* led by one of my mentors, Raymond Aaron. One of the ideas Raymond shared with us was the use of handwritten notes to acknowledge people in our lives. It could be a simple thank-you note, a birthday card or a congratulations card. I know how I feel when someone takes the time to send me a handwritten note. It always makes me feel special, so I decided that it would be a good idea to practice that simple exercise in my life. It only takes a few minutes, but the impact can be huge.

I taught the lesson of writing hand-written notes to my son Tyler at the young age of 13. During the summer of 2000, I was working at Fairbanks Ranch Country Club as the Golf Operations Manager. As an exclusive private club, many members preferred to walk and have a caddy. The caddy would carry their clubs, help with club selection and reading greens, and often provided good company and moral support.

I taught Tyler the basics of caddying over a few rounds of golf with me and he applied to be a caddy. That meant he would have to be at the club at 6:30 in the morning and put his name in the hat and hope for a job that day. When a member wanted a caddy, the Caddy Master would draw a name out of the hat and match a caddy with the member. Some days he would luck out and get drawn early. Other days he might have to wait a few hours. Some days his name did not get drawn at all. When he did get hired, the pay was good. Normally he would earn $40 for a round, or $80 if he caddied for two members at a time.

At the beginning of the summer, Tyler set out his financial goal. Every day when he got home, he would neatly lay out all the cash he had earned on his bed. He would separate the bills by 20's, 10's, 5's and 1's and count it all up. He would know daily where he stood financially and that seemed to inspire him. He was extremely motivated. Tyler consistently met his financial goals and to this day still keeps close track of his goals and his money.

One day I had an idea I felt could help Tyler out. Since I worked at the club, I had the membership list with the member's home address. I had Tyler sit down after every round and write a personal note to each member that hired him to be their caddy for the day. Here is a copy of a typical note that Tyler would send to a member.

Thank You Note

I am quite certain that was the first thank-you note any member had ever received from a caddy.

Tyler never wanted to take the time to write the notes, but soon things started to shift. After a while, members would call the Caddy Master in advance to say they had a tee time at 8:00 and requested Tyler to be their caddy. Wow. Now he would be guaranteed a job that day and did not have to show up for the caddy draw at 6:30 a.m.

About a month after Tyler starting writing thank you notes, one of the members found his way back to my office. He was an imposing man, standing about 6'6" and had an exceptionally large frame. He filled the doorway with his commanding presence. He was a litigation attorney and was used to getting his way. He was not the friendliest man and had a tough outer shell. My office was tucked out of the way of the Pro Shop, so it was most unusual for a member to seek me out. My mind started to wonder, *What's wrong?*

"I just stopped by to let you know that I received a thank-you note from your son, and it melted me like butter."

I was startled by what he said. Then he turned and left. I sat there awestruck at what had just happened. Obviously, that simple note had a huge impact in his life.

Even though Tyler was by far the youngest and least experienced caddy, it was not long before he became the most requested caddy at the club. A few years later while caddying for one of the members, Tyler shared that he was applying to Pepperdine University and was hoping to go there the next year. The member surprised Tyler by telling him that he was on the Board of Directors of that prestigious university and encouraged Tyler to apply.

As it happened, Tyler was accepted to Pepperdine. Even though we never found out if that man had any influence on his acceptance, taking the time to make that relationship could have played a vital role. And all it took was spending five minutes at the end of the day to send a simple thank you note. This is not a complicated or expensive marketing strategy, but without a doubt it is one of the most effective approaches I have ever seen.

I have carried the power of acknowledgment into our real-estate business. We have a team meeting every two weeks. Tyler is now an integral team member and has started leading the meetings. During our meetings we review what new properties have come up for sale, discuss changes in the industry, and make any announcements we have. The highlight of the meeting is the acknowledgements given by Tyler at the beginning of each gathering.

When we first started doing this a few years ago, it seemed that the same people were being acknowledged regularly. Several others at the table would just sit there with blank stares on their face with little to offer. Over time, those who weren't being acknowledged for excellent performance drifted away. We now have a core team that is fully engaged and at every meeting, each person at the table is acknowledged at least once, mostly for sales, but also for extra-special things they have done.

Sometimes the acknowledgment is for having the courage to walk away from business that did not fit with our company values. The acknowledgements section often takes a full 45 minutes. I believe this is the most important part of the meeting and has created an environment where everyone is fully recognized for the value they provide to our team. It seems that each week the acknowledgements section gets longer.

I believe firmly that people will do more for acknowledgment than money.

This chapter would not be complete without me sharing how important it is to not only acknowledge others, but to acknowledge the most important person in your life: YOU! I have a daily practice of acknowledging something I did that day. This daily practice continues to build my self-confidence. Not every day is filled with bliss and joy, but there is always something I can be grateful for and give acknowledgement to. It gets me through the challenging days and makes the good ones even better when I can carry that positive feeling forward to the next day.

What insights did I gain from these two experiences?

One of the greatest lessons I have learned is the "Power of Acknowledgment."

Taking the time to acknowledge others in a sincere way is one of the best ways to build friendship, loyalty, and trust.

There are many ways to acknowledge people, and the handwritten note is at the top of my list.

The art of a handwritten note has seemingly been replaced by today's high tech world of email, text messaging, and social media. These methods of communication are effective and certainly easier, faster, and less cumbersome than taking the time to hand-write a note. However, there is magic on the receiving end of a hand-written note. The fact that someone took the time sends a clear message that they really care. A text message or email simply cannot match a hand-written note. Try it and see the results for yourself.

If you want to start the practice of writing hand-written notes to acknowledge others, you may want to try these simple steps:

- The first step is to be prepared. I often found that when I wanted to send out a card, I didn't have the right card on hand. By the time I had a chance to go to the store and buy one, the opportunity had passed.

- Go to the store, or online, and stock up on all kinds of cards so you have them ready. A typical selection will include cards for these purposes: birthdays, anniversaries, congratulations, thank you, graduation, and sympathy. Get a bunch of blank cards, too, so you can personalize them for any occasion.

- If you want an excellent selection of high quality cards at great prices visit: www.SomeOfMeCards.com. I use them all the time and can highly recommend them.

206

- Get stickers, lots of stickers. It may seem cheesy but people of all ages love stickers. Buy hearts, smiley faces, and whatever else appeals to you. Then add one or two to each card and envelope.

- Buy a roll of stamps in advance so you are prepared. There is nothing worse than having to make a trip to the post office just to send out one card.

- Always hand-address the envelope. Never use a label.

- Try sending out one card a day. It takes just 5 minutes. At the end of the year, you will have touched 365 people. That is 365 people who will have a warm heart, and a smile on their face. Imagine the ripple effect you will have started.

P.S. Let me know how this worked for you and how you liked the book. My address is right at the front of this book. And yes, I love receiving hand-written notes . . . with stickers!

17

THE POWER OF A STREAK

Doing my push-ups at the top of Double Peak, San Marcos, CA

"We train our soldiers to go to war,
we don't train them to come home!"

– Steven "Chief" Kuryla,
U.S. Special Operations Intelligence Officer

On June 14, 2016, I was scrolling through Facebook and came across a post that caught my attention. It was my friend Tim Garlin, and he was doing 22 push-ups. *That's odd,* I thought. After he finished his push-ups, he said he was going to be doing 22 push-ups for 22 consecutive days and challenged everyone to do the same and post it on Facebook. Well, I am always up for a challenge.

At the time I was not at the level of fitness I was used to. I had been working long hours and let myself believe I did not have time for exercise. So, I decided to take it on. There is a mountain I can see from my office window in Lake San Marcos. I thought, *Why don't I do my push-ups at the top of the mountain each morning? That way I would really make an improvement in my fitness.*

The next morning, I headed up the mountain. The grade is steep, and the first 100-yards got me out of breath in no time. I had to take several breaks on the way up and I realized just how out of shape I was. It took at least 30-minutes to get to the top and I felt a real sense of accomplishment just doing that. Then I found a level spot to do my push-ups. *Twenty-two can't be that hard,* I thought. I was in for a big surprise. After only ten, I had to stop. I took a rest and did another five. Then I took another rest and did five more. Then I sucked it up and did the last two to complete the 22. It was not pretty, but I got it done. It was humbling to see how out-of-shape I was.

I resolved to never let myself go like that again.

The next morning, I took off on the journey again and once more those first 100 yards had me winded in no time at all. I got to the top and this time I cranked out 15 in a row, took a breather, and finished the last seven. Progress. I got back and posted it on Facebook and challenged others to do the same.

I was already feeling better about myself and I committed to keep going. I did have a question, though. "What was the significance of the number 22?" I reached out to a knowledgeable friend and she said it was the average number of veterans who committed suicide every day. I was startled, shocked and sad all at once. The 22 push-up challenge was to create awareness for this tragic situation. Suddenly, doing 22 push-ups took on a whole new meaning. It was no longer about me.

The next morning, I dedicated my 22 push-ups to the veterans who had committed suicide the day before. I had a new surge of energy. I visualized a veteran on each push upwards. Suddenly doing 22 push-ups seemed like a small feat relative to what our veterans have gone through.

Each morning, the hike up the mountain got easier, and the push-ups got easier, too. But on each trip up the mountain, I would wonder why so many veterans were committing suicide every day. More importantly, "What could I do about it?" It is a monumental problem, and it is happening all across the country. Yet the problem was being swept under the rug. Nobody was talking about it. Having no military background, or experience with suicide, I was in foreign territory. I knew I didn't have the answers and didn't even have any real idea what the source of the problem was. I do know that to solve any problem or make change in the world, it starts with making people aware there is a problem.

So, I made a commitment to increase the level of awareness about veteran suicide. I posted my journey each day on Facebook and people started to pay attention. I researched Post Traumatic Stress Disorder (PTSD) to understand it better because it was identified as one of the leading causes of veteran suicide. I knew that if I was not even aware of this problem two weeks ago, most of the population was likely oblivious to it as well.

As I approached the 22nd day of the challenge, I was feeling so much better physically. I felt it would be silly to stop my journey, even though the challenge was over. On day 22, I posted on Facebook that I had completed 22 days and challenged others to take it on. Many did. Then I asked, "What should I do next?" Someone suggested, "Keep going and add one more push-up a day."

What a great idea! I then challenged myself to keep going for 100 consecutive days. Every morning I was up the mountain and added one more push-up. Once I got to 50, I found that my form started to suffer so I broke it up into two sets and by the 100th day I was able to do two sets of 50. This was a massive improvement from the first ten I struggled with just 100 days earlier.

There were a few days in that 100-day stretch where I traveled to Las Vegas, and I found a different mountain to keep the streak going. There were days I did not feel like doing it. Some days were easy, and others were a real challenge. There were days when it was raining, and days that my body felt like it needed a rest. Whenever the going got tough, I would just think of what veterans had gone through and suddenly my task seemed trivial in comparison and it gave me new energy. Never once did I waver in my commitment.

Again, at the end of the 100th day, I asked myself the same question as I did on day 22. "What's next?" Now that I had the streak going, I did not want to rest even for a day and start all over again. I also noticed that I was feeling so much better physically, and I had boundless energy. Business had seen a marked improvement. In fact, it seemed like everything in my life was getting better. This wasn't a coincidence.

I remembered from my training for the IRONMAN Triathlon that as I increased my intensity, rest became more and more important. Doing the same thing over and over again was not always beneficial. After 100 consecutive days of climbing the mountain, I switched up my fitness routine, but kept the push-ups going.

I joined a gym and hired a personal trainer, and we began increasing the intensity of my workouts and added variety. I started the 22-push-up challenge at age 60. After a few months I felt like I was ten years younger. My trainer gave me a huge compliment when he told me he could not get a 35-year-old to do what I was doing.

As I said earlier, I was noticing benefits in other areas of my life that were not fitness-related. I developed a philosophy years ago that expresses my belief about the power of commitment:

"To develop power in your life, say you are going to do something and then do it."

I realized that somewhere along the way I had kind of let things slip in my life. I was no longer challenging myself. I was getting soft, both physically and mentally. So, thank you Tim Garlin, for challenging me. That one challenge turned my life around for the better.

As of February 21, 2021, my streak is at 1,733 consecutive days of doing at least 22 push-ups a day. In 2018, I did 24,000 push-ups.

In 2019, I did 36,500 and in 2020 I did 44,530 – that's 122 a day (100 for me and 22 for the veterans.) It is all recorded in the notes section on my phone. I still post on Facebook to continue to create awareness for veteran suicide, and to keep me accountable. Now that I have accomplished at least 22 pushups for so many years, the power of the streak gets stronger and stronger. I am commited to continuing the streak as long as I physically can.

Over the past four-plus years, there were days that were a real challenge to keep the streak alive. I had a bout of shingles that laid me up for two weeks. Later I fell on my rib and bruised it severely. That injury was extremely painful. For about ten days I could barely breathe while doing my push-ups and a few days I had to do them on my knees.

At the beginning of 2020, before COVID-19 was announced, I was extremely sick for at least three weeks. Although I was never tested, I am quite sure I had that disease. I lay in bed for three solid weeks, but I always took a few moments to get my 22 push-ups in. There have been times where I crawled into bed exhausted after a long day of work, only to remember I had not done my push-ups. I would get up out of bed and do them – no matter what.

Since I started this journey, I have done push-ups in three countries in a variety of settings. I have done them on the beach in Hawaii at the site of the IRONMAN. I have done them in minus 30-degree temperatures in North Bay, Canada on a frozen lake while wearing skates. I've done them in deep snow, wearing snowshoes. I have done them under the Olympic rings at Squaw Valley, California, in the desert heat of Palm Springs, California, at an elevation of 9,800 feet in Breckenridge, Colorado; on a fishing boat; on numerous golf courses; at a resort in Mexico; and pretty much wherever I am that day.

People often marvel at the commitment I have to this mission and ask where I find the time to do it. It takes me about 30 seconds to do 22 push-ups. This is about the time it takes to brush my teeth (which I have been doing quite regularly for more than 60 years.) It would be easy to minimize the achievement when comparing it to brushing my teeth, but I gain a huge amount of power from keeping a commitment I made to myself. It spills over to every area of my life. When I honor my word with one action it makes me stronger. By honoring this sacred commitment, I honor myself and I keep my integrity.

I believe that integrity is doing what I said I would do, even when no one is looking.

I have received so many benefits personally from this challenge, it is impossible to measure. The real reason I keep doing it though, is for the veterans.

The world needs to know this is a very real problem. As I have learned more and more about how many veterans commit suicide and why, I realize what a massive problem it is. I do my best to understand, but I cannot imagine the horrors of being in war.

The statistics are absolutely sobering. Just over 7,000 servicemen and women have died in combat since 9/11. During that exact same time frame, over 160,000 military veterans have committed suicide. That number is staggering!

This is not a simple problem to solve, and it is easy to look at the numbers as just statistics. But these are real human beings, tragically dying every day. Every death affects countless friends and their loved ones for years to come. These suicides are often due to the soul-crushing trauma they experienced while fighting for our freedom. They deserve better.

What can we do about it? As I said earlier, this is an extremely complicated problem with no easy answers. But I believe it all starts with awareness. The 22 push-up challenge is one way we can all participate. It's important for us to talk about it and show sincere appreciation to every veteran we meet, especially as we welcome them home. Who knows? The day we acknowledge a veteran may be the day they were planning on committing suicide and we could save a life by this simple act.

I could easily devote an enormous amount of time writing about veteran suicide, but that is not the purpose of this chapter. My intent is to illustrate how doing one small thing each day adds up to a huge difference by the end of the year. It is the consistency that is key.

I have learned so much from this simple exercise. The more I keep my word, the more power I develop. The strength I have gained from this push-up challenge has spilled over into everything I do. Beyond just physical strength, the streak has given me power I never thought I had. I know with 100% certainty I can count on myself to keep my agreement about doing at least 22 push-ups everyday – no matter what. That knowing has given me confidence that whatever I set out to do will get done. There is never any question about it anymore.

Writing this book is another example of consistency. Some days I didn't feel like I was making much progress. I just kept doing a little bit every day, and now almost a year and 77,000 words later, it is a finished book. That is the power of a streak.

At the beginning of 2020, our team at The Davidson Group Realty set a lofty goal to increase our business by 20% over our previous record year set in 2019. In the first month, our team fell from seven Realtors to five. In March, COVID-19 hit, and we had to make all kinds of adjustments to our business processes. No more open houses, no printed flyers allowed (to decrease the risk of spreading the virus), and in-person showings were dramatically limited. Yet even with the odds stacked against us, we surpassed our team goal on December 11. After a brief celebration, we sold seven more homes the week before Christmas, shattering our previous record in the process.

Was all this because I was doing push-ups each and every day? It sounds too simple and not even related. Actually, I believe this commitment is one of the main reasons for our success. It instilled a belief deep down in my core that anything is possible, and that belief has been picked up through osmosis by all our team.

I invite you to accept the 22 push-up challenge. Start today.

What insights have I gained from this experience?

The power of a streak is incredible.

The longer the streak goes on, the more power it develops. It is like having an accountability coach following me everywhere I go. The consistency of doing one thing, each and every day, has a multiplying effect by the end of the year.

The more I keep my commitments, the more integrity I develop.

The more integrity I have, the more people trust me. The more people trust me, the more they want to associate with me.

By declaring my commitment to others, it increases my level of accountability.

I keep track of my progress daily in a journal and I continue to post my progress on Facebook. That keeps me accountable to myself, and when I know I am accountable to others, it strengthens my resolve.

18
ASK FOR HELP...THE GREATEST GIFT

**With Janice – ready to deliver another load
of furniture to a deserving veteran.**

"You get in life what you have the courage to ask for."

– Oprah Winfrey

One day a young Marine was at our home, where we were in our garage loading up another U-Haul truck full of furniture, bedding, supplies, and food – the difference was this time it was for him.

When we were done, he thanked us profusely and, almost as an aside quietly said that he wished he had called sooner. I asked why he had not called earlier.

"I was given your phone number six months earlier. I just did not want to ask for help."

I was startled. I stopped him in his tracks.

"When you were active in the Marines, and your battle buddy asked you for help, how would you respond?"

The young Marine replied, "I would be happy to help."

"How did that make you feel?"

"It felt good to be able to help my buddy," he acknowledged.

Then I asked him if he had kids. He proudly let me know he had two young children. I asked how it makes him feel when they ask him for help.

A big smile came over his face. "It makes me feel so good."

I let him know how it made us feel when a young Marine like him asked us for help.

"We feel good that, in some small way, we could partially repay the huge debt we owe veterans and their families. You have all made tremendous sacrifices."

When that young Marine asked us for help, it was actually a gift to us.

I saw the light bulb go off in his head, as there was an immediate shift in his perspective. He understood that asking for help was not a sign of being a weak man, but rather was a gift to us.

I let him know that most of the civilian world wants to do something to help our veterans. We just do not know how. By asking civilians for help with a specific request, it truly serves them, too.

Somewhere in our culture we have developed a false belief that when we ask for help, it is a sign of weakness. In fact, it is quite the opposite. It gives others the joy of service.

Janice and I do a great deal to support veterans and we have noticed a common denominator among them. Veterans rarely, if ever, ask for help. I don't know if it is a pride thing, or an institutional value they adopt as part of their military culture, but it seems to go with the territory. It appears they would rather suffer than ask for help.

Along with the generosity of our real-estate clients and our community, we have completely furnished more than fifteen apartments for veterans. We have also provided food, clothing, and shoes to countless others. Whenever we put out a request to our community that a veteran needs help, the community quickly rallies and donates most everything that is needed, while we facilitate the delivery to that veteran in need. It is a win for everyone. Members of our community feel good, and veterans receive what they need.

In addition to asking FOR help, I have found that asking TO help can be just as powerful. In Chapter 18 of this book, The Power of Acknowledgment, I described my experience of helping my good friend Mark Wright in a time of need. When he described his situation, I immediately asked, "What can I do to help?" His initial response was that he was okay. I didn't take that for an answer, and I am sure glad I booked the next plane ticket and went to help. I know I made a difference in Mark's life, and I learned so much about giving and acknowledgement through that experience.

I have noticed that many people have a hard time asking for help, and equally as hard a time accepting help when offered to them.

In 1988, I was sitting in a seminar led by Mark Victor Hansen, co-author of the #1 NY Times Bestseller, *Chicken Soup for the Soul* series and *Ask! The bridge from your dreams to your destiny.*

Mark taught me that if I wanted something, I just had to, "Ask, Ask, Ask, Ask, Ask, Ask, Ask!" He would say it rapid fire, seven times. He would say it several times during the day and it always got a good laugh from the audience, but the way he said it has stuck with me ever since. I am forever grateful for the lesson Mark taught me. I would not be where I am today without that huge nugget of wisdom.

Mark also taught me to be specific in what I was asking for. If I made a vague request, it would be almost impossible to get what I really wanted. For example, let's say I needed one thousand dollars.

So, I go up to my friend and tell him I needed some money and ask for his help. If he pulled out his wallet and gave me one dollar, he did what he was being asked, but my real goal would not be satisfied. Of course, I could always ask a thousand people for a dollar – or I could just ask one person for a thousand dollars.

I also learned that when asking for help, my intentions needed to be pure and honorable. Along with that, I needed to be willing to do something in return, or even in advance.

I discovered that when I do ask for help, I often get it, even though sometimes I do not.

But one thing I know with 100% certainty: – if I do not ask, the answer is <u>always</u> "NO."

With experience in asking, I realized that if I don't get a "yes" answer the first time, it doesn't mean the answer will always be "no." Often, it just means that I need to get creative and ask in another way.

Here are just a few examples of the many life-altering experiences I have had, just because I had the courage to ask – often in creative ways.

1. I met Tony Robbins and spent a day with him as my mentor. I never gave up asking after being told there was no way Tony would have the time to meet with me. This one day was priceless and came to be because I was persistent and creative in how I asked.

2. I secured a job at the Ottawa Athletic Club, at a time when they were not hiring. I was willing to ask for the job and was hired ahead of many other candidates – because I offered a gift first – my services free for a full week.

3. I met Raymond Aaron – all because I asked him to buy an insurance policy, in the most creative way. Later Raymond asked me for help and together we created The Millionaire Club.

4. I manifested a job at Fairbanks Ranch Country Club because I asked for help. This gave me an incredible place to practice. Then I asked TaylorMade to sponsor me with the best

equipment money could buy. At the time, there were thousands of golfers who were more skilled and more deserving than I, yet I received their sponsorship because I asked them. Then, former LPGA golfer Lynn Adams agreed to be my coach. These three things were worth thousands of dollars, and yet cost me nothing – all because I asked Tag Merritt specifically what I needed to pursue my goal.

5. I am married to Janice, the best and most important ask of my life. The first time I asked her to marry me, the answer was not what I was looking for. Truth is, I was not ready for a "yes" answer at that point. When I was ready and asked again, she gave me an immediate yes.

As my friend Martin Rutte says, "You have to do it yourself, and you can't do it alone." If I can't do it alone, that means I need to ask others for help.

What Mark Victor Hansen says is so true: "Ask, Ask, Ask, Ask, Ask, Ask, Ask!"

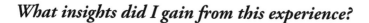

What insights did I gain from this experience?

Asking for help is a sign of strength, not weakness.

Asking for help is a gift to the person I am asking. Most people genuinely want to be of service to others and by asking them for help I give them that opportunity.

When I don't ask, the answer is always NO.

By asking for what I want, I have a chance at getting a "yes" answer.

When I don't get a "Yes" it is an opportunity to be creative and ask again.

It only takes a moment to ask, and the rewards can last a lifetime.

Just "Ask, Ask, Ask, Ask, Ask, Ask, Ask!"

I have learned that the quickest way to get something done is to ask others for help. I still occasionally fall back into old patterns and struggle with asking, thinking I might be a burden to others. Then I remember I am offering a gift by asking others for help.

19
BUYING A SLICE OF HEAVEN ON EARTH

The Welcoming Committee

"The precise location of Heaven on Earth has never been established, but it may very well be right here."

– Herb Caen, Columnist for the San Francisco
Chronicle, 1936 – 1996.

223

A s I walked around the side of the cabin, I was suddenly greeted by two majestic deer.

At first, they were startled by my unexpected visit. I, too, was surprised.

These two deer had the gentlest of souls and continued to stare at me for a long time. I suspect they were assessing me and wondering who I was, and why I was on their land. They were curious and did not seem at all afraid. We looked at each other for several minutes, with an incredible non-verbal communication going on between us.

I took this as a sign that they were the welcoming committee and had just given me permission to stay. Once their message was delivered, they turned around and disappeared silently into the woods. I knew I had found my Heaven on Earth.

One Monday evening in February of 2020, Janice and I were both up working late on our computers. It was about 11:00 p.m. Simultaneously, a real estate email flyer arrived in each of our inboxes. The headline was, "For Sale – 22 Acres with 3 Homes on Top of Palomar Mountain." The price had been reduced and the seller was motivated.

As Realtors, we get several emails like this each day. As most do not apply to us, they often get ignored. This one caught the attention of both of us. The number 22 resonated with me because of the 22 push-ups challenge I have been doing for so long to create awareness for the 22 veterans who commit suicide daily. I thought maybe this could be a place for veterans to come and heal – and just maybe save a life. What an incredible gift that could be. I got chills just thinking of the possibilities.

For Janice, the number 22 is very spiritual and is what caught her attention. As we were in separate rooms, I called out to her and asked if she got the same email. She was just looking at it, and she asked, "Where is Palomar Mountain? We should go see it." I looked up the address and found it was only 75 minutes away. I agreed, "Why don't we go look at it?"

We saw from the listing on the Multiple Listing Service it had been on the market for seven months and had three price reductions. As Realtors, we know that when a home has been on the market for so long and has had several price reductions, there is usually something wrong. It typically is either a bad location, there is something physically wrong with it, or it has been poorly presented and marketed.

The photos of the property did not portray its true beauty. There were only a few photos of the land. As there were three homes on it, the Realtor had three photos of different kitchens and a couple of other rooms, but it was confusing to tell which rooms belonged to each house. The photos were obviously not taken by a professional photographer, and the lighting was not good. Overall, the property was not presented in a positive light, which likely attributed to its length of time on the market.

Even with this poor presentation, something was drawing us to this property like a magnet, and we could not explain why. The next morning, I called the agent and got her voicemail. A few hours later she called back, and we made an appointment to view it on Friday. At no point before this had Janice and I ever discussed buying a second home for us. This was not even on our radar.

That Friday morning, we headed up to Palomar Mountain with our son Tyler, his fiancée Mandie, and Ed, a veteran who had been doing some work for us. Ed wanted to drive his new Jeep, so we all piled in and off we went. As we were heading up the mountain, Janice reminded us that if we liked what we saw, to be sure not to show any emotion to the other Realtor. As we drove on this switchback road up the mountain leading to the property, the views kept getting better and better. We could see for miles. Part way up, Janice broke the silence and declared, "Okay, we'll take it!" We all laughed. We were still miles from the property, but we all felt the same way. We were above the clouds and we could already feel how peaceful it was. There were no other cars on the road, and it was like the place was just waiting for us.

Views that go on forever

This property is in a gated community with 16 other homes, all with similar-sized lots. We met the Realtor's husband/assistant at the gate to let us in. We then drove a mile and a half on a private road through the Cleveland National Forest and continued to climb in elevation, eventually reaching 5,500 feet. It seemed every time we turned a corner the views got better. We finally arrived at the first home, named Ponderosa.

It is a traditional log cabin with all the cedar logs milled from trees on the property. The wood-burning stove was on, and the cabin was nice and toasty. We all instantly fell in love with this cabin. It is a magical place. We looked out the window to see a huge, mature oak tree with a place in the middle where you could just sit and meditate.

Interior of log cabin
(Matt Marshall Photography)

The mountain air was crisp and fresh.

After touring the first home, we walked 100 yards to the next one, called The Schoolhouse. At one time, this was a one-room schoolhouse located in San Marcos – 45 miles away. When a new school was being built, this structure was scheduled to be torn down. The owner of the property decided to have it transported up the mountain and then completely transformed it into a cozy cabin with one bedroom and a loft.

The Schoolhouse

The panoramic view from the rear balcony looks over the forest at another mountain range in the distance. It took my breath away. Not another house or neighbor in sight.

View from the balcony

Then we drove to the main cabin which has a soaring 22-foot high cathedral ceiling with natural cedar beams and tongue-in-groove pine planks in between. It has a direct line of sight across the mountain to the world-famous Palomar Observatory. I love the view so much, I have set up my writing desk in the loft that has two huge picture windows looking right at the observatory. I could not ask for a better place to write a book, and this cabin has become our own personal sanctuary.

We walked around the property with its massive oak and cedar trees all over. The most incredible granite boulders jut straight out of the land – some are more than 20 feet tall. It made me wonder what caused these huge formations to come out of the land. We could see several other flat meadows where more homes could be built if we wanted them in the future. We then discovered the property has its own well that pumps more than five gallons a minute into a huge holding tank. Palomar Mountain is famous for selling bottled spring water. Water never tasted better – right out of the tap.

As we walked to the pump house, we found a great storage room, a diesel back-up generator in case the power went out, and a huge Case tractor with a backhoe and shovel on the front. The more we discovered, the more we liked everything about the property. Again, none of this was even on our radar a few days earlier. Something just kept telling us we needed to buy it.

Then the messages started to come in. First there was the significance of the 22 acres. The address is 22668. The investment company we use to buy property has the number 16888 in front of it. All of this seemed pretty "coincidental." The next day, I called the Realtor to let her know we were interested and would likely write an offer, but we wanted to go up and see it again the next day. I asked her if there was a lockbox for the main gate so we could get in. She said, yes and gave me the combination. Miraculously the combination is the same number we have been using for years for our contractor lockboxes. I was curious to know what the chances are of having the same four-digit combination on a lockbox, so I did the calculations and found the odds are 1 in 10,000. It was like the universe was hitting us over the head with a 2x4 saying, "Wake up and just buy this."

As I mature, I have learned to pay greater attention to signs and patterns, instead of just treating them as coincidences. I remember when I was in my late twenties, I read a quote on circumstances by George Bernard Shaw, the winner of the Nobel Prize for Literature in 1925. His wisdom had a profound impact on me then and even more so now.

> "People are always blaming their circumstances for what they are. I don't believe in circumstances. The people who get on in this world are the ones who get up and look for the circumstances they want, and, if they can't find them, make them."

What I learned from that quote is that I am 100% responsible for my circumstances, and I can change my circumstances for the better at any time I choose. Janice and I were now in a situation where we could change our circumstance if we chose to.

We own other investment property that has tenants, and we had set some money aside in case another great deal came up for a rental-income property. We never know when that opportunity might present itself, so we had set aside a couple hundred thousand dollars just in case. It was sitting in a bank savings account, earning virtually no interest. That may seem foolish to some, as the money was idle, but our planning to have that money readily available made the difference between us being able to take advantage of this incredible opportunity versus just wishing we could.

First, we had to see if we could get a loan for the balance. This was not a typical rental-income property. The remote location and the fact that two of the homes did not have building permits added another dimension to the complexity of securing a loan. So we called our trusted lender, Liliana Riquer, to see if we would qualify for a loan by adding this to our portfolio as a second home, meaning we would not need rental income from it. When we got the green light from her, we wrote up an offer, and after a little negotiating we settled on a price.

Part way through the escrow process the underwriter wanted photos of each side of the main cabin. This was a most unusual request, one I never had in 17 years of selling real estate. As the other Realtor was not available, I decided to drive up on my own in the middle of the day. I arrived and as I walked around to the back side of the cabin, there were the two young deer staring at me.

If I had any doubts about this place, that encounter absolutely removed them. I took the photos I needed, but instead of driving back right away, I decided to stay a while. I laid on a huge rock and enjoyed the views and the many sounds of the forest and listened to the birds chirping.

Since we purchased it, we have been busy decorating it to our tastes. The insides have been completely repainted. Normally, I would hire one of our painters to do this work. In this case, I chose to do it myself with some help from Janice, Tyler, Mandie, and one of our trusted associates, Ben. Doing the painting has allowed me to really connect with the property and has been great therapy. We have upgraded the appliances, water heater, and made all the necessary repairs. We had our electrician install lighting that shines up at the cathedral ceiling, which really showcases that feature of the home and creates a soft warm hue reflecting off the pine. We had a crew of five professional tree trimmers here for six days trimming and removing trees that were either a danger to the house or interfered with the view. With all three homes being heated with wood-burning stoves, we now have enough firewood to last a few years.

As I stand here looking out over our land, I am reflecting on how far Janice and I have come in the last 25 years from renting our first place that was only 385 square-feet. I am humbled and so incredibly grateful.

I recall that after several months of living in that tiny space, we decided to find a bigger place and lucked out on a small guest house in Rancho Santa Fe. It was a Spanish-styled, adobe home designed by the famous architect, Lilian Rice. It was about 800 square-feet and was nestled under towering eucalyptus trees and some magnificent Queen Palms. At the time it was a big upgrade for us. We were flat broke and the rent of $800 a month was a huge stretch for our budget. I was struggling to send money back to Canada to support my kids. At the end of the month, we were always juggling which bill to pay first. I felt guilty moving into this bigger place and paying almost double the rent.

Although we have purchased our new property in the mountains, it feels more like we inherited it – that it was truly a gift to us. We are so grateful the Realtor did not do a good job marketing it, or someone else would have bought it six months earlier.

Today, I feel so incredibly fortunate to be able to receive this new property and feel good about it. There is no guilt and I feel truly deserving of it. Janice and I are still figuring out the many options for the best use of the three homes and land. As I indicated earlier, there is ample room to add more cabins to open all kinds of possibilities. The ground is extremely fertile, and we have excellent water, so we could set up greenhouses and grow whatever we want.

We have discussed using it as a retreat for veterans to allow them to heal. We could also turn it into a rental-income property, but something tells me there is a higher, more spiritual purpose for it. We have already used it as a place for our extended team who support our real estate business, and for special clients to come. It is our way of saying, "thank you."

I envision creating a Power from the Heart podcast series. It would be incredible to interview heart-centered authors, entrepreneurs, business leaders, and philanthropists committed to making a difference on the planet. We could invite them to come, spend a few days on the land, and have powerfully candid conversations with them in the log cabin. I can only imagine the wealth of knowledge and experiences that could be shared. It could be the start of a new chapter in my life and another way to give back.

Right now, I am just enjoying every minute of being here!

———⟡———

What insights did I gain from this experience?

Opportunities often arise when I least expect them.

We certainly never expected to buy a second home in the mountains. It was not planned or expected, but the opportunity was so incredible we could not pass it up. Having the courage to act on opportunities when they arise is what determines my outcomes.

I have learned to trust my intuition.

I recognize that I always have a choice to take advantage of opportunities that are presented. I pay attention to my gut feeling, and it rarely steers me in the wrong direction. It has been almost a year since we acquired this property and I can now say with 100% certainty, my gut feeling was right on.

By being prepared, I have the ability to seize opportunities when they arise.

Preparation takes planning, discipline, and sometimes short term sacrifices, and is one of the keys to success in life. Had we not saved up money for a down payment and established excellent credit to be able to qualify for the loan, we would not own this property now. This took years of preparation to be able to take advantage of this unique and fleeting opportunity, and ultimately it was well worth it.

Most of all, I am grateful for the abundance we have attracted, and I am happy to share it.

Regardless of the ultimate purpose of this magical place, I am so grateful to be able to share it for the highest good for everyone who has the joy of visiting our "Heaven on Earth."

20

THE RIPPLE EFFECT

The Ripple
(Artist: Ben Humbert)

"I hope I inspire others to do something good in the world."

— Bella Fleming, 6th Grade Student

This chapter is inspired by a letter I received from 11-year-old Isabella "Bella" Fleming. I have known Bella since she was a baby, and she and her twin brother Kinley are extraordinary children, largely due to the exceptional upbringing by their mother, Jamie Fleming. Both Bella and Kinley are wise beyond their years.

They are still kids at heart but can carry on a meaningful conversation with adults and are always a pleasure to have around.

Earlier in this book I shared with you the story of The Power of a Streak. This is just one of the ripple effects that came from the 22 push-up challenge. A ripple effect occurs when one event influences another. When you drop a pebble in a pond, the ripple created by it influences everything that comes in its way.

December 12, 2020

Dear Doug,

Last year you had a Walking with Warriors event and inspired us to take the 22 day push-up challenge to bring awareness to our country's daily Veteran Suicide rate. My family did this challenge together and we haven't stopped since. It is our daily reminder of how many people need help.

Last summer, during the pandemic, I learned how to crochet scarves while visiting my Grandma. One day when I was walking with my mom and brother, I told them how worried I was about the homeless I see every day and how cold they will be in the winter months. So I decided to make scarves for them. I shared my idea with you, and you encouraged me to not only make scarves myself, but to ask others to help me. I am excited to report that so far, we have 40 scarves and beanies made, $1,000 raised for additional items and lots of yarn to make more.

I hope I inspire others to do something good in the world. I really like this project and it is really fun.

Love, Bella

It is so exciting that an 11-year-old girl would be inspired to take on a project like this. It is especially refreshing, given the circumstances of our world during the summer of 2020. When Bella's Project was created, we were in the middle of a health crisis due to the global COVID-19 pandemic, millions were unemployed, the country was in political chaos, wildfires were burning over 4 million acres in California, protests and riots revolving around racial and social injustice were occurring daily, and suicide rates were surging.

For many, the multitude and magnitude of the problems may have seemed way too large to tackle even one of them. Watching the news was depressing. It would have been so easy to throw up our arms in resignation and cynicism, thinking, "It's hopeless. What can I possibly do as an individual? How can I possibly make a difference with all that is going on around me?"

Yet, here was one inspired young girl willing to stand up and declare she was going to make a difference.

While Bella's actions will not solve the many problems mentioned above, what I know for sure is that that at least 40 homeless people will be warmer this winter.

The ripple effects that will occur from her single declaration and her actions remain to be seen. But the lingering impact could be extraordinary, well beyond her efforts. For example, how will those homeless people respond from Bella's selfless gifts? Will they be inspired to do something kind for others? The ripple effect from her actions could potentially go on well into the future.

Bella has already inspired numerous people to donate money and supplies for her project. Many are also busy crocheting scarves and beanies. I wonder what goes on in their minds while they take the time out of their schedule to give back to others. Maybe their perspective on life and helping others is being shifted. Maybe they will be inspired to take on a project of their own.

Obviously, Bella's story has inspired me enough to write about it. She is a shining light.

Now thousands will read about Bella's Project in this book. How many readers will be inspired to start something wonderful on their own? How many more will share it with their friends?

The ripple possibilities are endless.

Isabella Fleming – crocheting another scarf

Since I finished writing the first draft of this story, Bella has been delivering her scarves and beanies in backpacks that include socks, toothbrushes and toothpaste, water, energy bars, and a blanket. The response has been extremely positive and has inspired Bella, and her brother Kinley, to take her project to the next level. Bella has now named her project Imagine I.F. (I.F. are Isabella Fleming's initials). She has increased her goal to helping 100 homeless people, and every day she is Imagining I.F., and what she can do to help those less fortunate. It is a way of life for them. Kinley has created an exceptional logo for her.

The word imagine has a special meaning for me personally. John Lennon's song *Imagine* resonates so well for me and Janice, we had it sung to us at our wedding. Now I can only imagine where Bella's project will go. I can only imagine what our world would be like if everyone shared the same values as Bella and Kinley.

(Artist – Kinley Fleming)

Another powerful example of the ripple effect that came from the Power of a Streak occurred on August 14, 2020, which happened to be our 22nd wedding anniversary.

Janice and I were made aware of a man named "Jack" who was going through some very dark times. Jack has served more than 20 years as an undercover police officer and witnessed many heinous crimes and like so many others in his line of work, the experiences took a huge toll. Alcohol was controlling his life. He had lost his job, was experiencing health challenges, his wife had left him, and his two boys were wondering who this person they called Dad really was.

Jack realized he was in a desperate situation. He had hit bottom and was ready to climb out of the big hole he was in. He committed to going through a rehabilitation program that caters specifically to veterans and police officers. He raised significant funds by selling some of his belongings to pay for this critical program. Jack was also given a partial scholarship, but he was still $5,000 short of what he needed, and the program was about to start.

A good friend made us aware of Jack's situation. Once he shared with us who Jack was and what he was going through, Janice and I immediately decided to gift Jack the remaining $5,000 he needed to attend. This was our anniversary gift to him. We called the rehabilitation center, made the payment, and Jack started the next day.

At that point we had not met or even spoken to Jack. All we knew was that our friend vouched for Jack and said his life was worth saving. We made the gift and sent him a blessing. We wished the best for him with no expectations. This was not a loan – it was a gift with no strings attached.

Then there was silence, and we had no idea how he was doing. We just kept sending positive energy to him.

About two months later we received a call from Jack. This was our first communication with him, and we spoke for over an hour.

He started by saying, "I cannot begin to thank you for what you did for me."

He thanked us profusely and then tearfully said, "You saved my life." His words were spoken with such sincerity we could tell he really meant what he said.

Nobody has ever said that to me before – it was a huge acknowledgment and came from his heart. We were instantly moved and touched by his words.

Janice and I encouraged Jack and emphasized, "You did all the work. We just helped facilitate."

Jack had completed the 45-day program and by then had been sober for 66 days.

During our conversation we asked what else he needed to rebuild his life. Being proud, and not wanting to ask for anymore help he told us he was fine. He offhandedly indicated that his car needed some repairs and was being held together with duct tape.

Miraculously, a few days later our friends Robby and Linda Adams called us and mentioned they had bought a new vehicle and had a pickup truck that was in good running condition. They wanted to donate it to a deserving veteran and asked if we knew of a worthy recipient. We said "absolutely," and connected them with Jack. Jack received his truck just after Christmas and the truck bed was full of food donated by our generous community.

Jack texted me on Christmas Day to say that this was the first time in years he has been sober for the holidays and that he and his family are so grateful.

Janice and I are happy to have made a gift to a complete stranger, having no idea of the outcome. While we initially thought we were just helping one person, we just don't know how far that ripple may travel. It starts with Jack's boys whose lives will be forever different. Who knows how their lives would have turned out if Jack had not turned his own life around? How many other lives will his boys touch?

The boys are also learning an important life lesson. No matter how hopeless circumstances seem at the time, they can always be turned around with one choice, followed through by action. What an inspiration their father is being for them.

Jack is employed again, and his smiling face, combined with his own inspiring story, will definitely have a positive effect on everyone he comes in contact with. Jack has already indicated he wants to be of service to others and be able to give back.

Jack texted me yesterday and proudly declared he has been sober 173 days.

The ripple possibilities are endless.

What insights did I gain from this experience?

The ripple effect is limitless in possibilities.

When I make an impact on one person's life, I am really impacting many others. What started as a 22 push-up challenge at a Walking with Warriors event, rippled into Bella's Project. The two projects were not related and yet one influenced the other.

The ripple effect just keeps going, and we have no control over how many people are positively impacted and in what ways.

When a pebble is dropped into the pond, it creates a ripple that keeps expanding beyond its initial impact. And then another ripple is created. Those ripples keep expanding outwards and affect every-thing they touch. Sometimes ripples will run into other ripples and have an even greater influence on each other (just like our friends donating their truck to Jack).

One person can impact the world.

Regardless of how hopeless the circumstances may seem, when one person like Bella steps up and drops a pebble in the pond, the course of life is altered forever. One person cannot solve all the problems of the world, but they can be a huge inspiration to others in so many ways. When enough people are aligned, the impact is enormous – and it all starts with one person. And one pebble.

It takes courage to make a declaration and act, yet you don't have to do it alone. People will rally to support you.

Making a big declaration to do something outside of the norm is not always easy. When your project is inspiring, people will rally and support you in ways you never thought possible. Stepping up and making an impact is definitely worth it. Bella definitely did that with her project, and I admire her for that.

We need more shining lights like Bella in the world.

21
MY TOP 10 INSIGHTS

The Light Bulb
(Ameen Fahmy on Unsplash)

"A moment's insight is sometimes worth a life's experience."

– Oliver Wendell Holmes, Sr. – American physician,
poet, and author, 1809 – 1894.

I was not given *The Life Manual* at birth – the one that gives the directions for how to live life to the fullest. No one gets one. I mostly learned through trial-and-error, and I certainly made my share of errors. Later on, I learned so much from the people that I admired and respected – people who had already done what I was looking to do. That saved me a lot of heartache and catapulted me forward in so many ways.

Now, whenever I need answers on how to deal with a situation, or which direction I want to take, I tend to look back at my experiences and the insights I gained. I have created my own *Life Manual,* so to speak. My manual is made up of my Top 10 Insights and acts as my personal guide. In addition to using my personal guide, I am never afraid to reach out to my closest friends and advisors and ask for help whenever I need guidance.

I hope my collection of stories and insights inspire you, and they can also be your guide as you navigate through your own roadmap on this wonderful journey called life.

Here are my Top 10 Insights (in no particular order):

1. **The most rewarding things I do in life are often the ones that look like they cannot be done.**

    My goal of becoming a professional golfer on the PGA Tour looked like it could not be done – and many people reminded me of that.

    Deciding to compete in the IRONMAN Triathlon World Championships at a time when I could barely swim and didn't even know there was such a thing as a racing bike, looked like it could not be done – and many people reminded me of that.

    Starting my own real-estate business at a time when I had no experience, looked like it could not be done. It was scary at times, but the rewards have been well worth the risk.

    Declaring I was going to be a professional speaker the day after completing The Dale Carnegie course looked like it could not be done – and my first talk was definitely jumping into the deep end with no lifejacket.

Now I can add to this list – achieving my goal of publishing a book. I had no idea how many steps are involved besides just putting my thoughts in writing. I had no knowledge of what goes into a cover design. I did not know the book had to be formatted differently for paperback, hard cover, e-book, and Kindle. I didn't have a clue about how to get it published on Amazon. Even with my marketing experience I was a fish out of water when it came to promoting the book.

I have taken on some massive challenges in my life with no idea how to accomplish them. Many I achieved, and some I did not.

It would have been a great deal easier if I knew in advance that I could not fail, and someone gave me a step-by-step manual for each challenge, guiding me every step along the way. But then that would have taken all the excitement out of it.

Part of the reward of achieving goals that look like they cannot be done, is the mere fact that they looked like they could not be done – and somehow, through lots of trial-and-error, I got it done.

Each time I achieved a goal that looked like it could not be done, it boosted my self-esteem immensely and gave me the confidence to take on the next one. What also increased my confidence was setting small daily goals and then accomplishing them. The goal-achievement process is like building a muscle through weight training. Each time I would lift a weight I would get just a tiny bit stronger, but over time I increased my muscle strength tremendously. More importantly I built the strength of my mind as much as my body along the way.

2. I don't have to have all the answers before I take on a big goal.

Here was my reality. The day I decided to compete in the IRONMAN I had no idea what I was really getting into. There was no manual. As I went through my journey of training, I did not know if what I was doing was going to be enough to get me to the finish line.

As I stood on the beach in Hawaii, waiting for the race to start, I had many doubts. I had never swum 2.4 miles before and had done all my training in the pool. I had never put all three events of that distance together. At that moment, after 20 months of training, I still did not have the answer as to whether or not I could do it.

Almost twelve hours later, I finished it. I answered my question, "Could I do it?" with a big "YES!" Here is the interesting thing though: even after finishing the race, I still wonder how I did it. I have come to the realization that knowing how I accomplished it is really not that important.

What I learned from my IRONMAN experience is to stop looking for the answers in advance of pursuing a goal. I set my goal and I take the first step forward and make the many, many adjustments along the way. I systematically break the big goal down into manageable pieces and take on one obstacle at a time.

The journey is never a straight line from start to finish. I know I will get there sooner or later – as long as I never quit. Knowing this truth, deep in my bones, frees me up to go after things I would never think possible.

I have noticed that many people shy away from setting big goals because they feel the need to have all the answers before getting started. They paralyze themselves even before they start. Sometimes not knowing what is needed in advance is a blessing, otherwise accomplishing the big goal may be too overwhelming. There is magic in trusting our ability to take the first step and figuring it out along the way.

3. **Regardless of my current situation, I am in total control of the choices I make to determine my future.**

I started out in life with low self-confidence. As I set my goals, and then achieved them, my confidence grew and grew. I realize that no matter where I start, it is ultimately the choices I make, and the actions I take, that determine where I finish.

I have made many mistakes and had to completely rebuild my life from nothing – three times. I have learned that I have the ability to make different choices and control my outcome.

Successfully going through those painful rebuilding periods builds confidence. Now I have an inner-knowing that no matter how bad things get, I am always in charge of my destiny.

4. **Things move at light-speed when I am fully committed.**

I have learned that when I am fully committed to something, the universe quickly provides everything I need.

The story of how quickly I met Raymond Aaron, my first millionaire client, after deciding to sell insurance to millionaires is a perfect example of things moving at light-speed when I am committed. What resulted was beyond my wildest expectations.

The speed at which The Millionaire Club came into being is another example of extremely fast manifestation. It went from being just a thought in my head at 2:00 a.m. to a fully committed plan later that day. The entire experience was head-spinning.

All the pieces that fell into place when I decided to play golf on the PGA Tour happened within a few short weeks of making the declaration and asking for help. By being committed to something specific allows for the Law of Attraction to support me and manifest everything I need to support me.

5. **If I don't ask, the answer is always no.**

This might be the most powerful insight of all.

For example, the young Marine who asked us for help ended up receiving so many things he needed, just because he asked for them.

If I didn't ask to meet Tony Robbins, I never would have had the opportunity to have extensive one-on-one time with him and ask any question I wanted. It took some creativity, and it all started with me asking for what I want.

Sometimes when I do ask for something, the first answer is "no." If I keep asking for what I want and continue searching for how to receive it, eventually the answer will become yes. Sometimes I just need to be a little more creative in order to get what I am committed to receiving.

6. **Take responsibility when things go wrong and allow for corrections to be made.**

It is only when I take full responsibility for my actions that I can make a positive change.

This might include resolving a disagreement with another, or having others willing to work with me toward a common goal. Or it may even be realizing that I messed up, big time. This requires, me to acknowledge it and apologize to those I may have affected.

Blaming others for my circumstance does no good. I alone created them, and it is up to me to create the circumstances I desire.

Blaming others for my circumstance also turns me into a victim and takes all my power away. Once I own the situation, I can be responsible and make a change.

7. **The willingness to do whatever it takes is a fundamental key to success.**

Whether it be in business serving a client, or doing something for myself, my willingness to do whatever it takes determines my success.

Often, I won't be asked to do something, but my willingness to do it sets me apart from all my competitors — who for the most part are somewhat lazy.

This is an attitude I carry with me everywhere I go. This attitude just oozes out of the pores in my skin. You will never find me asking someone to do something I have not already done or am willing to do myself.

8. **Choosing who I spend time with greatly influences the outcomes in my life.**

The saying, "Show me your friends and I will show you your future" sums up this insight.

Spending time with people who inspire me charges my batteries. They help get me fired up and as a result I can do more with my life.

I also believe that if I inspire someone else, they get a positive charge, and everyone benefits.

In addition to being inspired by others, there is so much I have learned by carefully observing the actions successful people take. This applies in all arenas in life from business, athletics, health, relationships, and everything else you can name.

9. **The power of a streak is incredible. The longer the streak goes on, the more power it has.**

By saying I am going to do something and then doing it, I gradually and systematically develop power in my life.

By doing something daily and keeping track in a journal, I become accountable to myself. Sharing that goal or streak with others makes me even more accountable.

On the days that I don't want to continue – and believe me those days come up – the thought of breaking the streak gives me the strength to complete my task.

As the streak gets bigger the power also grows. As I write this chapter, (on February 10, 2021) my streak of doing at least 22 push-ups a day is at 1,722 days – almost 5 years). The thought of breaking the streak and starting over again always overcomes the feeling of "I don't feel like doing them today."

Through determination and commitment, I have proven to myself that I can accomplish amazing things. What is most interesting is how doing at least 22 push-ups a day has had such a profound impact in many other areas of my life, including business. At first glance, it isn't apparent there is a connection between my doing 22 push-ups a day and having record sales each year since I started this. But I believe there is a direct correlation. I believe that by creating such a strong discipline in one area, that discipline naturally spills over to other areas of my life.

10. **One person can impact the world.**

Regardless of how hopeless the circumstances may seem, when one person like Bella steps up and drops a pebble in the pond, the course of life is altered forever. One person cannot solve all the problems of the world, but they can be a huge inspiration to others in so many ways. When enough people are aligned, the impact is enormous – and it all starts with one person, one pebble.

There is no question there are many challenges facing the world – it seems like there are more today than ever before. Michael Jackson sings in his song Man in the Mirror, *"If you want to make the world a better place, take a look at yourself and then make a change." It seems so simplistic, but in reality, this is the best advice I have ever heard. It all starts with each of us.*

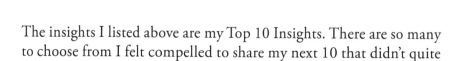

The insights I listed above are my Top 10 Insights. There are so many to choose from I felt compelled to share my next 10 that didn't quite make the list. The next 10 are extremely powerful, just like the first 10.

11. **Opportunities are presented to us all the time – often when we least expect them.**

12. **One of the greatest lessons I have learned is the "Power of Acknowledgment."**

13. **Asking for help is a sign of strength, not weakness.**

14. **A single act of compassion has the ability to affect a person's life forever.**

15. **By being prepared, I have the ability to seize opportunities when they arise.**

16. **All people deserve to be treated as equals.**

17. **I am capable of doing way more than I think I can.**

18. **The ability to speak in public is a learned skill – it is not something we are born with.**

19. **When I set a big goal, the assistance I receive often comes from the most unexpected sources.**

20. **Honoring my time commitments is the same as honoring my word.**

22
WHAT'S NEXT?
FOR ME... AND FOR YOU

Looking ahead
(Artist: Ben Humbert)

"Be the change you want to see in the world."

– Mahatma Ghandi,
world-renowned nonviolent Indian nationalist

Congratulations – you have made it to the end of the book. This action tells me you are someone who completes things you set out to do.

I trust that many of my stories, and insights, have ignited your soul. Now here is where the magic can happen, and it all depends on how you are inspired to act. I invite you to use these stories to take action. I wrote this book to inspire you into action – to make a difference in the world.

I would like to share some of my goals with you. Just as I described in earlier chapters, publicly commiting to my stated goals helps keep me focused and accountable.

WHAT'S NEXT FOR ME?

I am in a place of complete gratitude and peace. I am grateful for all the successes I have had in my life. I am also grateful for all the mistakes I have made. As painful as they were at the time, they have all been learning experiences and taught me that I can overcome any obstacle put in my path.

I am approaching 65 years young. This is often a time when people start their well-earned retirement after 45 or more years of working hard and saving. I now find I am more and more inspired every day. I have plenty of gas left in the tank. I know I have so much more to contribute.

Writing this book gave me a chance to explore all of the facets of my life. I relived many accomplishments I am immensely proud of. I also saw times where I made decisions that did not work out well at all. Reliving some of those poor decisions was painful, but also provided a healing experience. What did I learn from both my successes and my failures? What did I discover that could help make what is next for me even better? The important lessons from all the events of my life were my biggest takeaways.

The answer to the question of what's next for me is constantly evolving. I know for sure that I strive to make a lasting contribution to this world – to leave a lasting legacy. This book is just the start of my contribution. Where it will take me is yet to be determined, just like the Ripple Effect I described in an earlier chapter.

I do have some immediate goals I have identified for myself. As I have shared earlier, when I set a goal and share it with others it makes me even more accountable. I will do as I teach and share them with you.

1. Continue to improve my health and fitness daily so I have a finely tuned vehicle that will support me for many years to come. That includes doing a minimum of 22 push-ups every day – no matter what.

2. Create the *Power from the Heart Podcast*. I will engage with heart-centered experts and positive social influencers. Some guests will be household names. Others will be ordinary people who have overcome extraordinary odds to achieve uncommon results. The common denominator will be that each person will have made a positive difference in the world. I visualize this podcast being a beacon of light and inspiration. Feel free to recommend people to be interviewed.

3. Create a new Facebook group called, *Power from the Heart – The Positive News Channel*. This will be a place where members can go daily for inspiring news. It has always amazed me that 95% of the news on television is bad news. When we feed our mind with negativity it is impossible to stay positive. I choose to create an alternate source of news – one that inspires, creates, and attracts more good news

4. Have this book become a best-seller in the first month of publication and sell over 1,000,000 copies within 18 months from release. I certainly don't have the answers to how I am going to make this happen. As I have demonstrated throughout my book, having all the answers before starting a journey is absolutely not necessary. I don't need to know how I'm going to achieve my goal before I begin.

5. Be interviewed by Oprah Winfrey on her *Super Soul Sunday* program.

   I don't have a direct connection to Oprah, and she does not know me – yet. You may be familiar with the six degrees of separation. That is the idea that all people on average are six, or fewer, social connections away from each other. Here is where I am asking for your help. Please refer me to anyone you know who may know someone, (or someone who knows someone) to help me establish a direct connection to Oprah – hopefully with a recommendation. Or if you do know her personally, even better. I will take it from there. As I shared earlier – if I don't ask, the answer is always "no".

   Why Oprah Winfrey? First and foremost, it would be a tremendous honor to be interviewed by her. There are many people who have great talk shows, but Oprah is different from everyone else. She is in a class all of her own. Oprah's spirit is pure. She is one of the most giving people I know, and she lives by example.

   She also has an incredible following of people who are already making a difference in the world. That is the audience I would like to speak to – to be able to ignite their souls. In one hour with Oprah, I can make a huge difference in the world. Please help me to make this goal come true. I can already visualize sitting with her and sharing this paragraph. What better example to teach people that you can have what you want, just by asking for help, and following up with action?

WHAT'S NEXT FOR YOU?

That is a question only you can answer. You already know what lies within you and what you would like to do. However, sometimes our aspirations get buried deep in our soul – I know. It took me almost 20 years to have the courage to take on my goal of playing golf on the PGA Tour. It was buried so deep I had almost forgotten about it. What matters most, though, is not how long it takes but that we act on our goals, so we can achieve them. We ultimately desire to live our lives to the fullest. We want to look back on what we've done and be proud of how we took on all the challenges as we strove to make our dreams come true.

I trust you have enjoyed reading my stories, and they have ignited something in your soul. I trust my insights have been thought-provoking and given you practical tools to develop your own Power from the Heart.

No matter where we are in our own life, there is always room for growth. Jim Rohn, author of *The Art of Exceptional Living*, teaches, "For things to change, first I must change."

With that in mind, I invite you to consider a few challenges to take on, for yourself, and for our world.

1. Take on a challenge that stretches yourself. It may be something you have always wanted to do and didn't know where to start, or maybe it is something you were afraid you might fail at. Remember we don't have to have all the answers before we set our goal. Just make a commitment, take that first step, and figure it out along the way. This is where the excitement is – and soon you will be living life fully with passion.

   I recently listened to Tony Robbins interviewing Pitbull, the Cuban–American rapper, also known as "Mr. Worldwide." Pitbull openly shared about his humble beginnings and his worldwide success. He also spoke candidly about one of his schoolteachers, Hope Martinez. She taught Pitbull, "The biggest risk you take, is not taking one." He took her advice to heart and he hasn't looked back. Some wise words indeed.

2. Do 22 push-ups a day for 22 consecutive days. At the end of 22 days, assess how you feel and decide if you wish to continue. If you are inspired to do so, post your video on Facebook to create awareness for the tragic veteran suicide situation, and challenge others to do the same. Tag me when you post it, so I can cheer you on. The Ripple Effect of this one action is enormous. (If 22 push-ups are too much on the first day – as it was for me – break it up into smaller numbers

or do them on your knees until you build up your strength). Then observe how that simple exercise starts making a difference in every aspect of your life.

3. Create a project to do something good for the world. Let's face it, we are all in this together. The more attention we put on doing something for others, the more rewarding our lives become. Your project doesn't have to be elaborate. Just look for a problem out there and create a solution – like Bella did by making scarves for the homeless to help keep them warm in the winter. There is no shortage of problems that need solutions.

   If you are not up for creating your own project, simply find an existing organization that is addressing a problem you are passionate about and volunteer to assist. Whichever direction you go, just know you are making a difference in the world, and the Ripple Effect will reach farther than you can ever imagine.

4. Donate to a worthy cause. Don't do it for the tax write-off. Do it because you want to. I have learned that money is energy. When we hang on to it, it stops flowing to us. When we donate, in addition to helping the recipient person or organization, it also has the effect of having money flow back to us – often from unexpected places. When choosing where to donate, look at where your money will have the most impact. It can be an individual or an organization.

   Remember that when we leave this planet, we can't take anything with us. Denzel Washington once said, "I have never seen a hearse going to a funeral with a U-Haul being pulled behind it." Put your money and possessions to the highest good – and the more money you have, the more good you can do for our world.

5. Smile at strangers. Open doors for others. Give drivers the right-of-way. Treat everyone as an equal. And above all else: Be Kind.

I am deeply grateful and appreciative to have shared my life with you through this book. If any of the stories have been an inspiration and catalyst to create, dream, and bring forth your passion and purpose in your life, I would be genuinely interested in hearing about it. Please write and let me know what contribution you are making to the world. Who knows? Your story may be featured in my next book! Keep on shining your light.

I wish you peace, joy, happiness, fulfillment, and success in your life's journey. Live from your Heart – that is where your Power is!

LET IT SHINE

"Our deepest fear is not that we are inadequate.

Our deepest fear is that we are powerful beyond measure.

It is our light, not our darkness, that most frightens us.

*We ask ourselves, 'Who am I to be brilliant,
gorgeous, talented and fabulous?'*

Actually, who are you not to be?

You are a child of God.

Your playing small doesn't serve the world.

*There is nothing enlightened about shrinking, so that people won't
feel insecure around you.*

We were born to manifest the glory of God within us.

It is not just in some of us;

It's in everyone.

And, as we let our own light shine

we unconsciously give other people permission to do the same.

As we are liberated from our own fear,

our presence automatically liberates others."

- Marianne Williamson, author of Return to Love

ABOUT THE AUTHOR

Doug Davidson
(Jill Jones Photography)

Doug Davidson has led an extremely full and varied life.

Doug was born and raised in Montreal, Canada. In his early teens, he lived in Nigeria for three years with his family and spent one year on his own at an all-boys boarding school in England. He graduated from the University of New Brunswick with a BPE degree (Bachelor of Physical Education) in 1979.

An accomplished athlete, Doug played on seven sports team in his senior year in high school and was awarded Athlete of the Year. He played football at John Abbott College and volleyball at the University of New Brunswick. In 1982, he placed in the top 20% at the IRONMAN Triathlon World Championships in Hawaii – out of 900 competitors.

In his twenties, he overcame a lifetime fear of speaking in public and become a highly sought-after motivational speaker. He then started a seminar business, wrote a course called *7 Steps to Marketing Mastery*, and taught entrepreneurs how to market themselves effectively on a shoe-string budget. That led to him become a business and personal success coach, long before coaching became a popular career.

At age 44, he dropped everything to pursue his dream of playing golf on the PGA TOUR, and for two years that was his primary focus in life.

In 2003, Doug earned his real estate license. He was completely disenchanted by the lack of professionalism in the industry and decided to re-define the level of service to create a new standard. He owns, along with his wife Janice, The Davidson Group Realty – a thriving business with a team of five dynamic Realtors who consistently sell more than 50 million dollars of real estate each year.

Becoming a best-selling author is Doug's latest success story – and he is passionate about sharing his wealth of life experiences and insights. He is developing a podcast series where he will be having conversations with heart-centered leaders on a variety of topics. Doug and Janice are also developing a sanctuary on top of Palomar Mountain, CA, where guests and small groups can gather to nourish their souls, while creating new ways to have a positive ripple effect around the world.

Doug is available for podcasts and zoom meetings to share how to bring Power from the Heart into your life and those you care about.

For more information on the author, programs offered
by Power from the Heart, and the upcoming podcast series :
Power from the Heart: *Conversations with Heart-Centered Leaders*,
visit: www.PowerFromTheHeart.net.

Doug can be contacted at: Doug@PowerFromTheHeart.net.